Urban Transformation

Transit Oriented Development and the Sustainable City

Ronald A. Altoon
James C. Auld

images
Publishing

Published in Australia in 2011 by
The Images Publishing Group Pty Ltd
ABN 89 059 734 431
6 Bastow Place, Mulgrave, Victoria 3170, Australia
Tel: +61 3 9561 5544 Fax: +61 3 9561 4860
books@imagespublishing.com
www.imagespublishing.com

National Library of Australia Cataloguing-in-Publication entry
Author: Altoon, Ronald A.
Title: Urban transformation : transit oriented development and the sustainable
                 city / by Ronald A. Altoon and James C. Auld ; edited by Nancy Egan.
ISBN: 978 1 86470 457 0 (hbk.)
Subjects: City planning.
                 Transit-oriented development.
                 Sustainable development.
Other Authors/Contributors:
                 Auld, James C. Egan, Nancy.
Dewey Number: 711.4

Production by The Graphic Image Studio Pty Ltd, Mulgrave, Australia
www.tgis.com.au

Pre-publishing services by United Graphic Pte Ltd, Singapore
Printed on 140gsm Chinese Matt Art paper in Hong Kong/China

IMAGES has included on its website a page for special notices in relation to this and our other
publications. Please visit www.imagespublishing.com.

Contents

PREFACE

Years ago Ronald Altoon and I were both part of the Urban Land Institute (ULI) Awards of Excellence committee. While we jostled over ideas a bit there, he persuaded me with his broad experience and cheerful smile. He is one of the few designers who always listened, understood, and sympathized with my developer woes trying to build Transit Oriented Developments (TODs). He "gets" my frustration with transit engineers who think mobility and community-building are mutually exclusive—or make it that way. He and his partners have been in the trenches with community groups that want all the amenities of a compact neighborhood, but fight density to the death, never understanding that one is dependent on the other. They have struggled with developers helping them to see the long-term viability of a project, and, accordingly, invest in better design and higher quality materials.

In developer circles, my reputation fringes on the quixotic because of a decades-long, outspoken passion for creating neighborhoods around trains. This is still new terrain for US real estate developers are generally skeptical. They are curious as to how I can publicly advocate these notoriously difficult and often unprofitable projects with a straight face. This is foreign territory to them as they are just sticking their toe in the waters of our new economy and demography. In contrast, Ron's enthusiasm and can-do approach are a relief.

His careful explanations of the layers of complexity underpinning the design work of the firm has been informative. Beauty, economics, functionality, efficiency, community, marketability, and excitement co-exist equally in his vocabulary and descriptions. Many times the nuances of designs produced by Altoon + Porter have shifted my thinking, and Ron's insights and recommendations are almost always on target.

Recently I started noticing how many of the firm's transit-oriented designs were for projects outside the US. Producing quality TOD in the United States is still difficult. Walkable destinations around transit stations are so common in other countries that the US

shortfall is a bit perplexing. Certainly, the demographic trends and market forces suggest the need for more mixed-use districts and transit choices, but there are formidable challenges. Transit itself is just getting reintroduced, in fits and starts, several generations after the demise of streetcars. Low-density, single-use development has been easy in a country with so much land and space. Moreover, for over 50 years the financial rewards for sprawl development have been substantial. The public sector is beleaguered by organizational silos, eradicated budgets, and dearth of a long-term view. The American culture prioritizes capitalism over vision, while resistance to change is a fact of humanity. Unsurprisingly, project leadership and community support for TOD remain scarce.

The national TOD portfolio is accordingly small and, by and large, embarrassing. There are few truly integrated, walkable, transit districts. Transit facilities are often done at the lowest possible cost, focused on engineering efficiencies, with minimal consideration for customer experience and human sensibility. As a result, there are precious few great transit places, little variety in the ones we do have, only rare examples of development profitability, and consequently, minimal motivation for our industry and our communities.

Urban Transformation is really about providing that critical inspiration. It is about restocking our weak architectural portfolio of transit facilities with dynamic new models. It is about recognizing the potential value and longevity of these projects, and making them exceptional rather than forgettable. It is about using the "people hose" that transit generates to support private enterprise, diverse uses, and sustainable destinations. It is about leveraging a transit project into a transit district and into a healthy new neighborhood. It is about helping communities everywhere compete in the global marketplace.

The powerful cases in this book remove the excuses for mediocrity and mundane functionality, and shows us how to excel. The text introduces an understandable typology of development around transit, and uses that to illustrate different strategies and design techniques. There is a broad range and scale of projects represented—large and small, domestic and global, big markets and modest communities—and each an excellent example of what can be realized.

There are numerous examples of how good design can save rather than cost money, and indeed, how it can yield greater profitability despite higher capital investment. The projects repeatedly illustrate how to increase density, add diversity of uses, tighten connectivity and wrap it in a "wow" design to generate more revenue for the developer. This approach simultaneously increases ridership for the transit agency, launches a stronger brand and economic base for the community, and offers an attractive experience for travelers, workers, residents, shoppers and visitors. In short, *Urban Transformation* provides a new level of aspiration to the entire industry.

The timing could not be more perfect. The rush is really on to win waning monies for transit systems, most frequently seeking economic development and private investment around the stations. Hundreds of new stations, intermodal centers, and transit districts are being planned for a variety of transit modes—commuter rail, light rail, street car, bus rapid transit, high-speed rail, and more. New models and inspirations are critical if these facilities are to achieve the ambitious promises and goals of the community.

We must not resort to our old models and engineering solutions that prioritize vehicles over people. The transit must work well, of course, but there is much more to be accomplished, and to a large extent, the quality of the design will parallel the ridership and commercial success of the project. This is new world thinking for most transit agencies, which tend to focus on the cost of transit rather than its revenue potential. New opportunities abound, now, as communities seek projects and investments that provide environmental, economic and social benefits. TOD is perfectly positioned to deliver on that requirement—if done correctly—and

this book smashes through the minimums and shows us how to deliver exceptional places.

Finally, despite the depth of content, the images do most of the talking. Almost everyone loves a picture book, so telling the story via design is a terrific way to communicate. Implementation must be guided by a vision. *Urban Transformation* offers rich visions of transit that is beautiful, sustainable and catalytic to great neighborhoods. May it give you the confidence to smile when others suggest that you are tilting at windmills, and simply insist that we can reach much higher and achieve much more.

Marilee Utter
President, Citiventure Associates

INTRODUCTION

Let's begin with the irrefutable facts. There is a migration of people from the countryside into urban centers on every continent, and a consequential and unhealthy dependency on oil to power private vehicles, which have become the primary means of transportation. Additional cars, which emit carbon monoxide and deplete oxygen, produce pollution and unhealthy living conditions in many cities. The working poor, middle class, and wealthy each navigate through increasingly dense and congested urban cores. Despite a commitment to increased mobility, government at all levels appears unable to consistently and adequately fund public transit systems to mitigate the increased demand. Implementation of city planning schemes is delayed for want of public transit systems that would enable fulfillment of thoughtful civic visions. Many public agencies operate under annual deficits, and bureaucratic culture has been traditionally challenging for creative private sector initiatives.

In the context of this dilemma, Public Private Partnerships (PPPs) have emerged as a means of realizing urban investment in difficult economic times. The private sector has stepped in to partner with the public side to achieve compatible goals, bringing solutions that enable both the financing of public plans and associated private development. Successful partnerships depend on each side having clearly articulated goals and the talent and leadership to see them through.

Transit agencies have several goals. First, they want to optimize value from the real estate they control. Second, they have a mandate to increase the use of public transportation, reducing the use of individual private vehicles. Third, they want to make the Transit Oriented Development projects (TOD), promoted by the private sector, as attractive as possible, and to encourage multi-modal options where practical. Fourth, they want to encourage higher density on parcels adjacent to and in the neighborhood of transit stations, which, in turn, encourages people to walk to transit.

To achieve these outcomes and spur the best possible projects, transit agencies develop design guidelines with the assistance and approval of staff and professional consultants. Before large-scale transit systems can be put in place, municipalities need appropriate zoning and clearly defined entitlement processes. Political and local neighborhood support will be critical and needs to be nurtured. In general, transit agencies seek the best fit for each unique community where they locate a transit station and TOD, and evaluate the options that best satisfy the criteria within the specific context of the community.

Some agencies prefer to complete real estate transactions with long-term leases utilizing a Joint Development Agreement (JDA) document, which defines its expectations. In this case, the ground lease provides restrictions for changes over time in ownership, land use, tenants, operations, maintenance and so forth. As the transit agency provides information on the transportation element and its program expectations, it should also have a commitment to play a sustained support role in the entitlement process.

Transit's expectations of the private sector contribution include providing the type of development agreed to in the JDA and a professional process. Changes proposed by the developer that enhance projects are evaluated and accepted. A wise agency seeks the developer's best practice expertise in order to obtain the most comprehensive, thoughtful project; one that is tailored to the constraints and ambitions for a particular site. To further assure success, transit agencies often seek outside advice, including private sector planners, economists, and legal counsel.

A major issue in free-market, democratic countries is how to bridge the divide between public sector, social obligations, and private sector economic requirements. In many cases, transit agencies view the provision of transit stations as a value-creating real estate opportunity, with which they can generate additional capital to fund future land acquisition, entitlements, engineering, and construction of an expanding urban transit network. They generally focus less on the considerable added cost transit stations impose on real estate development, including noise, vibration, construction scheduling, building over an operating station or line, security and the like.

On the private sector side, the financing of projects—the product of a formulaic evaluation of land, pre-development, design, consulting, and construction costs against the projected income—often takes into account the "normal" building costs and parking required for such a development. The complexity of building over or even adjacent to transit stations brings added costs over conventional building, and likely a more complex entitlement process, both of which need to be budgeted.

The major challenge for the private sector developer is to find an equity investor, who will normally seek a return in excess of fifteen percent. Beyond this capital infusion, the developer will borrow the necessary balance from banks. If the project performs financially, the developer at-risk is rewarded for the five to seven years of work and the associated costs.

Throughout the process, it is critical the developer assure the adjoining neighborhoods that the development is appropriate for the context and will satisfy local demands and that it complies with planning regulations. Additionally, the developer needs to be certain the development program provides the necessary financial metrics to meet investor and banking requirements. Finally, the developer must to be confident that the investment will be attractive for another owner, should the project be sold in the future.

The one instrument the public sector can manipulate is the one that costs them nothing. Increasing the entitled, buildable area on transit station land or private sector land adjacent to a transit station, which can be achieved through up zoning, can increase the value of developing a TOD parcel. This has the potential of offsetting some of the additional development costs to the developer, making the project viable. If a developer could double or triple the development on a given parcel, the land cost diminishes in proportion to other costs, and the pro-rated balance can be applied to offset imposed transit-related expenditures.

Into this challenging situation comes the opportunity to develop single- and mixed-use real estate projects situated to take advantage of and encourage greater use of public transit systems in subtly differing ways. They fall into various categories. In addition to transit station design, this book will present several different prototypes that the authors have labeled for clarity: Transit Oriented Development (TOD), Transit Adjacent Development (TAD), Transit Environment Districts (TED), Transit Induced Development (TID), and Development Induced Transit (DIT). While transit agencies and advocates tend to look skeptically at non-TOD transit associated developments, there are many examples of such developments having been significantly altered in program composition or parking demand, as a direct response to transit proximity.

As collective world culture embraces the values of a green evolution, urban dwellers will feel compelled to alter their personal values to embrace sustainable working, living and mobility technologies. Cities and the development community have the opportunity to partner together to accelerate this evolution.

Ronald A. Altoon, FAIA, LEED AP

ACKNOWLEDGEMENTS

This book is the result of the passage in 2008 of Measure R, a ballot initiative in Los Angeles County, whereby citizens, faced with climbing gas prices and a declining economy, realized that public transit was the only way to assure mobility in this vast region. Unwilling to rely on the commitment of the Federal or State governments to serve a demonstrated need with sustained consistency, they voted by a majority greater than 67 percent to tax themselves an additional .5 percent on sales tax for the next 30 years to raise $40 billion to build out a comprehensive public transit system of rapid buses, light rail, subway, and heavy metro rail trains.

Once home to the most extensive public rail system in the world, which was demolished by collusion between transportation industry titans and a former misguided mayor, the city of freeways and freeway congestion was the last place on the planet anyone would have imagined a civic revolution on the issue of mobility. An exotic car culture seemed not to be able to support such an idea.

In 2010 the Urban Land Institute Los Angeles (ULI LA) District Council produced a TOD Summit that raised the issue to a high level of public awareness. This created the impetus to continue to focus on this critically important subject matter.

The authors wish to thank the following people, who gave selflessly of their time and intellectual capital to sustain this critical issue in the public realm, contribute their thoughts to the dialogue contained herein, create the diagrams and drawings, and challenge the assumptions.

Marilee Utter, Citiventure Associates, LLC, has been a collaborator in spirit at the Urban Land Institute's Public Private Partnerships Council, which advises on both public policy and private development for transit projects.

Roger Moliere, Chief of Management and Development for Metro, the Los Angeles County Metropolitan Transportation Authority, has been an inspirational leader in the public interest, shepherding the process of creating civic spaces while serving the public mobility needs, and has freely expressed his expectations and identified the internal and external challenges agencies like his face on a daily basis.

Paul Keller, Principal of Urban Partners, a successful TOD developer, was most helpful in synthesizing the issues both public and private sector leaders face. His courage to be a pioneer and resulting insight were invaluable.

Katherine Perez, Executive Director of the ULI LA District Council, who was instrumental in supporting the establishment of the ULI LA TOD Summit, has energized the discussion of mandating responsible development above, adjacent to, and nearby transit stations, as have members of the ULI LA TOD Committee.

Special thanks goes to Nancy Egan (New Voodou) for her invaluable editing of our text; A+P partner William Sebring for contributing project experience; Deirdre Stearns and Rebecca Brennan for bringing organization and clarity to the information, images, maps, and diagrams; and Andre Helfenstein, Francisco Arias, Luis Rodriguez, Joshua Koelewyn, Taylor Goodrich, Huijuan Yao, Joost Hulshof, Tymon Ros, Gregory Keating, Mat Yeung, Jessica Jiang and Richard Kuei for creating consistent, legible drawings.

Lastly, appreciation goes to our clients, whose civic commitment to Transit Oriented Development of many descriptions helps to assure the vision for a more sustainable world.

NOVOSIBIRSK, RUSSIA
NOVOSIBIRSK MIXED USE

NIZHNIY NOVGOROD, RUSSIA
COMMERCIAL COMPLEX

MOSCOW, RUSSIA
THE ATRIUM AT KURSKY STATION **118**
MOZAIKA (THIRD RING) **140**
MOSKVA COLLECTION **76**
YASENEVO **122**
ODINTSOVO

KRASNOGORSK, RUSSIA
KRASNOGORSK MIXED-USE CENTER

RADOM, POLAND
GALLERIA STONECZNA

DUISBURG, GERMANY
MULTI CASA CENTRAL STATION REDEVELOPMENT

LEEDS, UNITED KINGDOM
UNION PARK

GLASGOW, SCOTLAND
BUCHANAN GALLERIES **130**

AMSTERDAM, THE NETHERLANDS
MIXED USE PROJECT

UTRECHT, THE NETHERLANDS
NIEUW HOOG CATHARIJNE **108**

ROTTERDAM, THE NETHERLANDS
MIXED-USE PROJECT

GHENT, BELGIUM
THE LOOP **148**

BRUSSELS, BELGIUM
CHARLEROI STATION HUB MASTER PLAN **158**

CHODOV, PRAGUE, CZECH REPUBLIC
CENTRUM CHODOV **68**
MUCHA CENTRE **84**

BRNO, CZECH REPUBLIC
BRNO CAMPUS CENTER **136**

BRATISLAVA, SLOVAKIA
THE PORT

ST. ETIENNE, FRANCE
CENTRE DEUX

REDMOND, WASHINGTON
REDMOND TOWN SQUARE **174**

GRESHAM, OREGON
GRESHAM STATION **88**

SAN BRUNO, CALIFORNIA
THE SHOPS AT TANFORAN **114**

LOS ANGELES, CALIFORNIA
PICO / SAN VICENTE **48**
HOLLYWOOD & HIGHLAND **60**
GRAND AVENUE
BROADWAY PLAZA
MCA UNIVERSAL OFFICES
ONE WILSHIRE
SOUTHWESTERN UNIVERSITY LAW LIBRARY

LONG BEACH, CALIFORNIA
SHORELINE GATEWAY
PACIFICENTER/DOUGLAS PARK

SAN DIEGO, CALIFORNIA
FASHION VALLEY CENTER **162**

HONOLULU, HAWAI'I
WAIKIKI BEACH WALK

TORONTO, ONTARIO, CANADA
TORONTO UNION STATION **64**

BUILT ─────────□
IN DESIGN/UN-BUILT ─ ─ ─ ─ □
FEATURED CASE STUDY

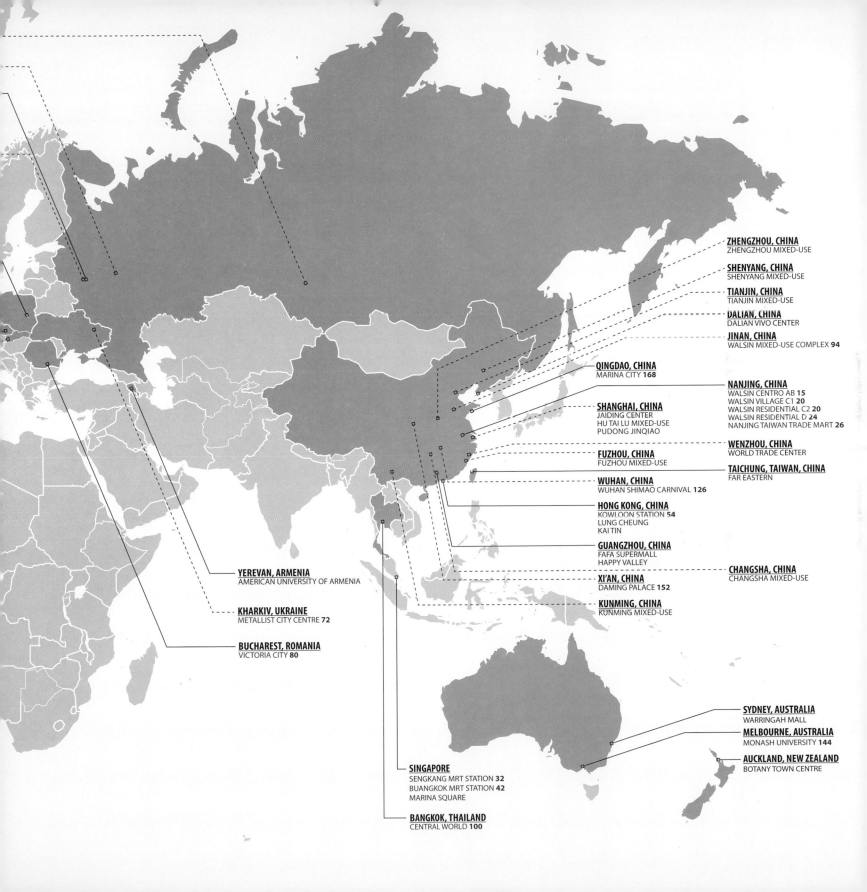

ZHENGZHOU, CHINA
ZHENGZHOU MIXED-USE

SHENYANG, CHINA
SHENYANG MIXED-USE

TIANJIN, CHINA
TIANJIN MIXED-USE

DALIAN, CHINA
DALIAN VIVO CENTER

JINAN, CHINA
WALSIN MIXED-USE COMPLEX **94**

QINGDAO, CHINA
MARINA CITY **168**

NANJING, CHINA
WALSIN CENTRO AB **15**
WALSIN VILLAGE C1 **20**
WALSIN RESIDENTIAL C2 **20**
WALSIN RESIDENTIAL D **24**
NANJING TAIWAN TRADE MART **26**

SHANGHAI, CHINA
JIADING CENTER
HU TAI LU MIXED-USE
PUDONG JINQIAO

WENZHOU, CHINA
WORLD TRADE CENTER

FUZHOU, CHINA
FUZHOU MIXED-USE

TAICHUNG, TAIWAN, CHINA
FAR EASTERN

WUHAN, CHINA
WUHAN SHIMAO CARNIVAL **126**

HONG KONG, CHINA
KOWLOON STATION **54**
LUNG CHEUNG
KAI TIN

GUANGZHOU, CHINA
FAFA SUPERMALL
HAPPY VALLEY

CHANGSHA, CHINA
CHANGSHA MIXED-USE

YEREVAN, ARMENIA
AMERICAN UNIVERSITY OF ARMENIA

XI'AN, CHINA
DAMING PALACE **152**

KUNMING, CHINA
KUNMING MIXED-USE

KHARKIV, UKRAINE
METALLIST CITY CENTRE **72**

BUCHAREST, ROMANIA
VICTORIA CITY **80**

SYDNEY, AUSTRALIA
WARRINGAH MALL

MELBOURNE, AUSTRALIA
MONASH UNIVERSITY **144**

AUCKLAND, NEW ZEALAND
BOTANY TOWN CENTRE

SINGAPORE
SENGKANG MRT STATION **32**
BUANGKOK MRT STATION **42**
MARINA SQUARE

BANGKOK, THAILAND
CENTRAL WORLD **100**

Walsin Centro
Nanjing, China

In conjunction with the 2008 Beijing Olympics, the Nanjing municipal government envisioned a major new Hexi development area to be master planned and constructed over time in the district adjacent to and surrounding the new Olympic Stadium. Broad tree-lined avenues set the urban framework and infrastructure for this new development area.

The master plan envisioned multiple high-rise office towers, retail centers, hospitality venues, residential developments, and a new convention center, along with public parks and cultural facilities. Central to this vision was the extension of the subway system and bus service which would connect the Hexi District to the heart of Nanjing and the new high-speed rail linkage to Shanghai and Beijing.

Walsin, a Taiwan-based industrial and development company, was selected to develop five contiguous sites. These projects serve as case studies that demonstrate the subtly different transit-related development types as they fall into three distinct categories.

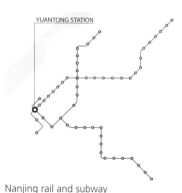

Nanjing rail and subway

15-minute walking distance

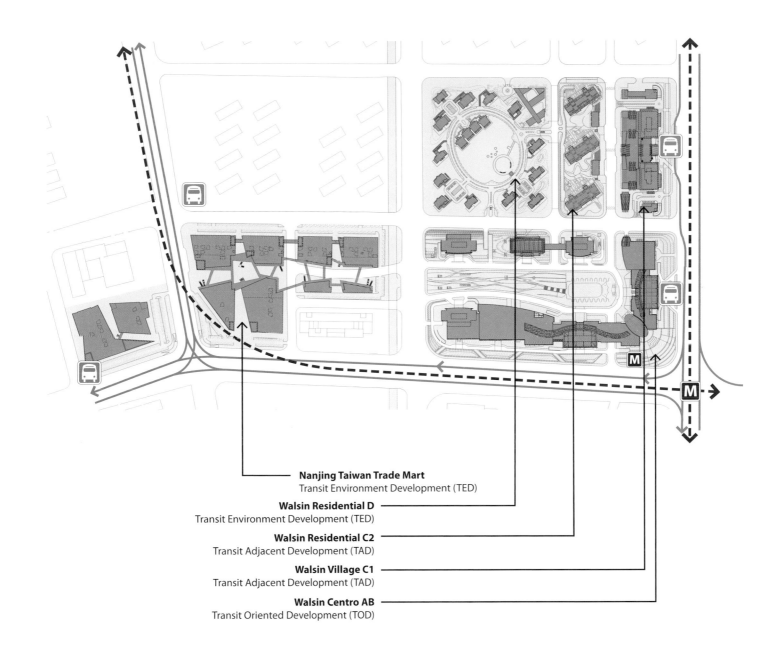

Nanjing Taiwan Trade Mart
Transit Environment Development (TED)

Walsin Residential D
Transit Environment Development (TED)

Walsin Residential C2
Transit Adjacent Development (TAD)

Walsin Village C1
Transit Adjacent Development (TAD)

Walsin Centro AB
Transit Oriented Development (TOD)

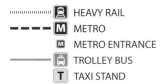

🚆 HEAVY RAIL	
Ⓜ METRO	
Ⓜ METRO ENTRANCE	
🚎 TROLLEY BUS	
Ⓣ TAXI STAND	

🚌 BUS STOP
🚌 BUS STATION
🚲 BIKE LANE/BIKE STORAGE
🚈 LIGHT RAIL
▸ TRANSIT/PEDESTRIAN LINKAGES

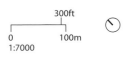

300ft

0   100m
1:7000

WALSIN CENTRO SITE PLAN

Walsin Centro Site AB

TOD

Transit Oriented Development projects are customarily situated directly above a single mode or multi-modal transit station. The 8.5-million-square-foot (2,590,800-square-meter) Walsin Centro AB mixed-use project—with office, hotel, serviced apartment, retail, entertainment, leisure, dining and civic uses—which is linked directly to a subway station falls into this category. The Walsin Centro AB project is the touchstone of the overall development area.

Walsin Village Site C1/Residential Site C2

TAD

Transit Adjacent Development projects are located on sites contiguous to, but not above, transit stations. The Nanjing C1 office/retail mixed-use development and the C2 residential complex directly across the street are such sites. Connected at the concourse level to the subway station, and at the surface to major bus lines, they are considered to be transit adjacent.

Nanjing Taiwan Trade Mart

TED

Transit Environment District projects are located in an area within half a mile of a subway or light rail station and a quarter of a mile of a bus stop. The Nanjing Taiwan Trade Mart—which encourages cross-Strait, business-to-business trade between China and Taiwan—is such a project, as is the Hexi site D residential compound close by.

Walsin Residential Site D

Project point of entry from the subway system

Walsin Centro AB

Public Sector Needs

In an effort to accommodate the explosion in urban migration to Nanjing, and to create a new satellite downtown area for the city, the planners envisioned that the Hexi District would accommodate all forms of development residential, office, retail, hospitality, cultural, sports, recreation, education, and convention. In order to enable this development, an expansion plan for the subway and bus systems was to be implemented, along with significant road and infrastructure improvements. Anticipating market demand, city planners also sought the involvement of the private sector to develop large-scale projects with world-class designs. The private sector would have to embrace the bold vision without demographic data to support their investment.

Private Sector Needs

The first of a multi-block master development, the Walsin Centro AB mixed-use project was designed for a site directly contiguous to the Yuan Tong metro station, which accommodates both the east–west and north–south lines. Accessed directly from concourses below and above ground, the 7-million-square-foot (2.13-million-square meter) complex includes office towers of 58, 50, 23 and 22 stories in height; a 41-story five-star international-class hotel; conference facilities; seven levels of retail, cinema, dining and leisure; as well as two landmark civic spaces. In order to realize this ambitious project, which the city had planned without a thorough vetting of the dimensional and service needs of the building types, the developer required significant public sector flexibility to accommodate alternative

Civic park

visions. Bus stop locations and engagements also required negotiation, but the dealing with metro planners was primarily administrative.

Project Issues

Mandated by the city, a large central park connecting visually to another, larger civic park one block away was negotiated with significant compromise from both the public and private sectors. Setback lines were prescribed, necessitating further negotiation. In addition, another requirement limited building coverage to 45 percent, mandating 35 percent landscape coverage. The requirement to use a government LDI (local design institute) with limited experience in highly complex, sustainable, mixed-use projects, challenged collaboration on a myriad of design issues, yet resulted in a project of strong design sophistication.

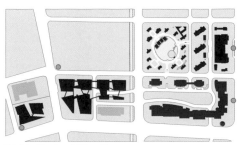

Walsin Centro AB location map

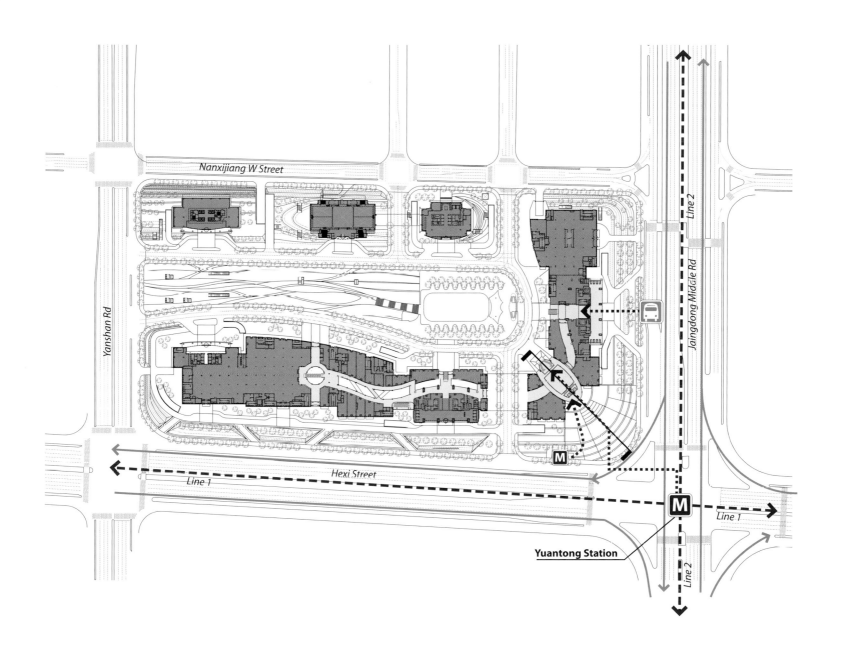

Nanxijiang W Street

Yanshan Rd

Hexi Street

Line 1

Line 1

Jaingdong Middle Rd

Line 2

Line 2

M

Yuantong Station

▦ HEAVY RAIL		🚌 BUS STOP	
Ⓜ METRO		🚍 BUS STATION	
Ⓜ METRO ENTRANCE		🚲 BIKE LANE/BIKE STORAGE	
🚎 TROLLEY BUS		🚈 LIGHT RAIL	
T TAXI STAND		▸ TRANSIT/PEDESTRIAN LINKAGES	

150ft

0   50m

1:3500

WALSIN CENTRO AB SITE PLAN

Aerial view

Design Solutions

The design team began with the transit station and bus stop locations as force vectors, which allowed the project to be crafted around the movements of public transport users. Office buildings, the hotel, conference center and retail amenities face the central park. The powerful orthogonal perimeter façades facing the streets, six-story high oval trellis defining the grand atrium at the point of entry from the subway system, and curvilinear building fronts facing the park, all combine to create a yin–yang relationship, and a clear definition of the relaxing nature of the public park.

Public Benefits

The project embraces the central public park, directing the view and attention of the subway and bus riders towards it, as a visual and participatory amenity. The transit system delivers people first to a series of public spaces, and then into the private-sector commercial complex. A full range of urban amenities, in a Rockefeller Plaza-like setting, allows residents, neighboring communities, office workers, sports enthusiasts and convention delegates easy access to goods and services normally found only in downtown central business districts—all in a clean, safe and pleasant environment that fulfills public sector goals.

The grand atrium

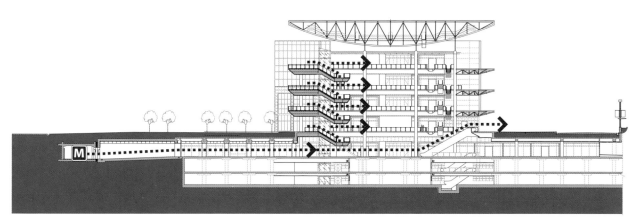

⊟ HEAVY RAIL	⊟ BUS STOP	
Ⓜ METRO	⊟ BUS STATION	
Ⓜ METRO ENTRANCE	⊡ BIKE LANE/BIKE STORAGE	
⊟ TROLLEY BUS	⊟ LIGHT RAIL	
Ⓣ TAXI STAND	▪▪▪▪▶ TRANSIT/PEDESTRIAN LINKAGES	

75ft
0   25m

WALSIN CENTRO AB GRAND ATRIUM SECTION

Retail/dining village

Walsin Village C1/Residential C2
Public Sector Needs

The project is located one block north of the Yuan Tong subway station, which prompted the public sector to seek a convenient, all-weather concourse connection from the site to the station. Additionally, they wanted immediate access to bus stops located across a landscape buffer, which was a part of the city's avenue design standard. Although existing landscape regulations did not allow passage through the buffer, city planners wanted the regulation waived to allow direct pedestrian access to the two office towers and retail center. With direct access, designated surface pedestrian

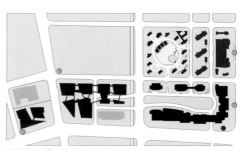

Walsin Village C1/Residential C2 location map

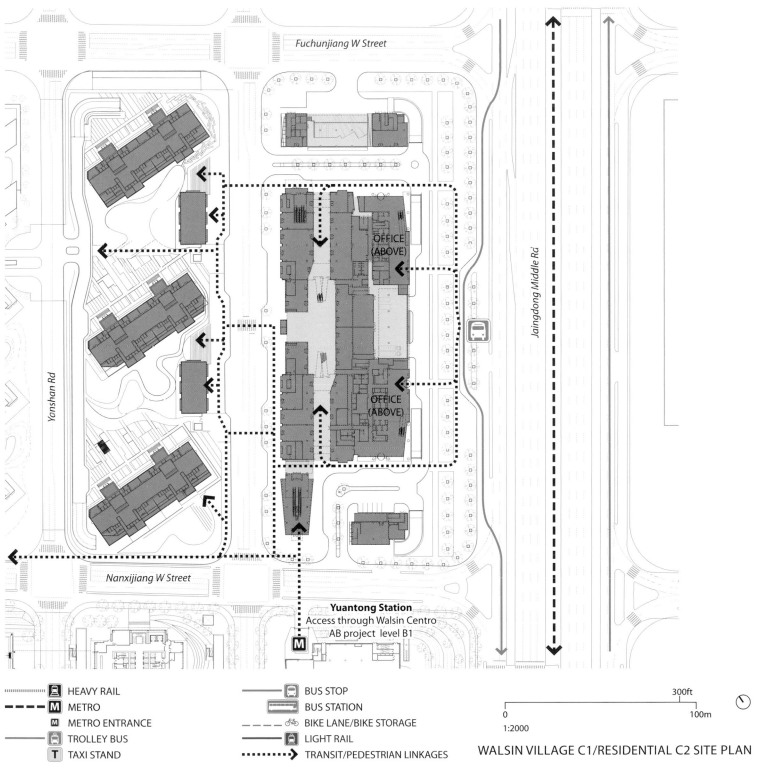

Fuchunjiang W Street

Jaingdong Middle Rd

OFFICE
(ABOVE)

OFFICE
(ABOVE)

Yonshan Rd

Nanxijiang W Street

Yuantong Station
Access through Walsin Centro
AB project level B1

Ⓜ

⬚ HEAVY RAIL		🚌 BUS STOP	
Ⓜ METRO		🚌 BUS STATION	
Ⓜ METRO ENTRANCE		🚲 BIKE LANE/BIKE STORAGE	
🚋 TROLLEY BUS		🚈 LIGHT RAIL	
Ⓣ TAXI STAND		▸▸▸ TRANSIT/PEDESTRIAN LINKAGES	

300ft

0 _____ 100m

1:2000

WALSIN VILLAGE C1/RESIDENTIAL C2 SITE PLAN

paths could easily connect the six-tower Walsin Residential C2 complex, located directly west across the street, to the Village site.

Private Sector Needs

The developer, Walsin, sought and received public sector approval of a concourse that would run under a public street, to connect the Walsin Village C1 site to the lower ground level of the Walsin Centro AB site. From there, immediate, all-weather access could be provided to the subway station. In addition, pedestrian pathways that crossed through the landscape buffer at convenient points would connect to designated bus stops.

Project Issues

As designated by the city's master plan, the two Village sites were restricted in critical east–west dimensions. The long, narrow mixed-use site, which could be accessed by vehicles in only two locations, would contain two office buildings, multiple restaurants, and retail shops, all of which require separate, hidden service dock functions. Established setbacks were confining but had to be observed in the design, while the city required a project with strong visual identity on all four exterior elevations to provide a positive impact.

Design Solutions

Utilizing a lower level concourse to link to the adjacent Walsin Centro AB site, it was possible to create a seamless flow of pedestrian movement from one property to the other, and on to the public transit station. Above the concourse, a three-level, open-air, retail/dining village is protected from the wind and sun by the building massing and high trellises. Iconic "lanterns" mark the ends of the retail passage. Two 14-story corporate office towers face internal arrival streets as well as the major Jaingdong Middle Road anchoring the project. Pedestrian paths provide linkages, which continue through the Walsin Village C1 site to provide direct connection to the Walsin Residential C2 complex across the street. Access to two modes of public transit includes one all-weather connection to two subway lines.

Public Benefits

Designed in concert with the Walsin Centro AB site, Walsin Village C1 and Walsin Residential C2 offer the benefit of a complementary, alternative shopping/dining experience. Designed as an open-air environment rather than an enclosed galleria, it expands offerings at a more moderate price point, to further attract greater ridership on the public transit lines.

Aerial view

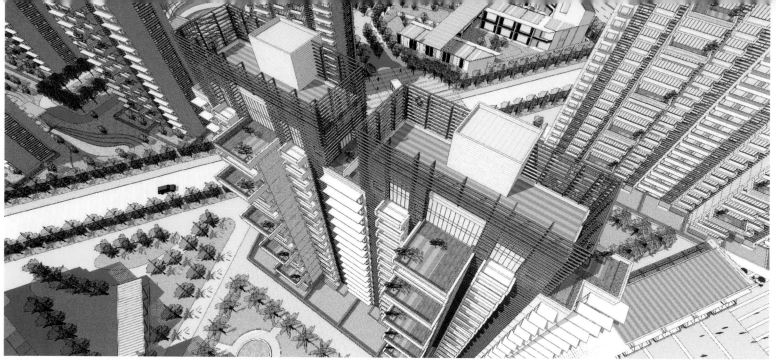

Aerial view of residential towers

Walsin Residential D

Public Sector Needs

The master-planned residential complex of 13 high-rise towers and lakefront townhouses was designed to accommodate the growing migration of people from villages and farms to China's major cities. Parking was required in support of the apartment units. However, because of the proximity to the transit station and bus lines, the developer wanted the city to accept a lower number of parking spaces than the market would have suggested had the project been located a further distance from public transit.

Private Sector Needs

In return for the city's acceptance of reduced parking, Walsin would provide a range of amenities that would make the project more engaging, including a man-made lake constructed over subterranean parking, which would create a visual and recreational focus. Taken with the entirety of the Walsin Nanjing contiguous developments, the total project would be a living environment where every need would be satisfied without the use of a personal vehicle.

Project Issues

Chinese city planning codes require that a specified number of hours of daylight strike the windows of every room of every unit in residential buildings. Accordingly, buildings angled in the east–west direction to the noonday sun are the most efficient in satisfying this requirement. However, the rectangular site was not aligned with respect to the solar orientation that would most efficiently satisfy this requirement. As a consequence, this put a greater burden on the planning of the project, making it more difficult to satisfy even the reduced parking requirement on site.

Design Solutions

The resulting scheme, on axis with the bias of opposite corners of the site, responds to the challenge of orientation with the secondary benefit of directing pedestrian movement along the edges of the lake to the corner of the site, which is most convenient to the subway and bus service on the main avenue. The towers, landscape and man-made lake all sit above a lower level parking structure and recreation center, creating a park-like environment for all residents to use and view from their units.

Public Benefits

The location of this large-scale residential development in a transit district clearly reduces the need for personal vehicle use. Residents have easy access to facilities that provide for their daily needs in the greater project area, and to rapid transit to all parts of Nanjing and cities beyond.

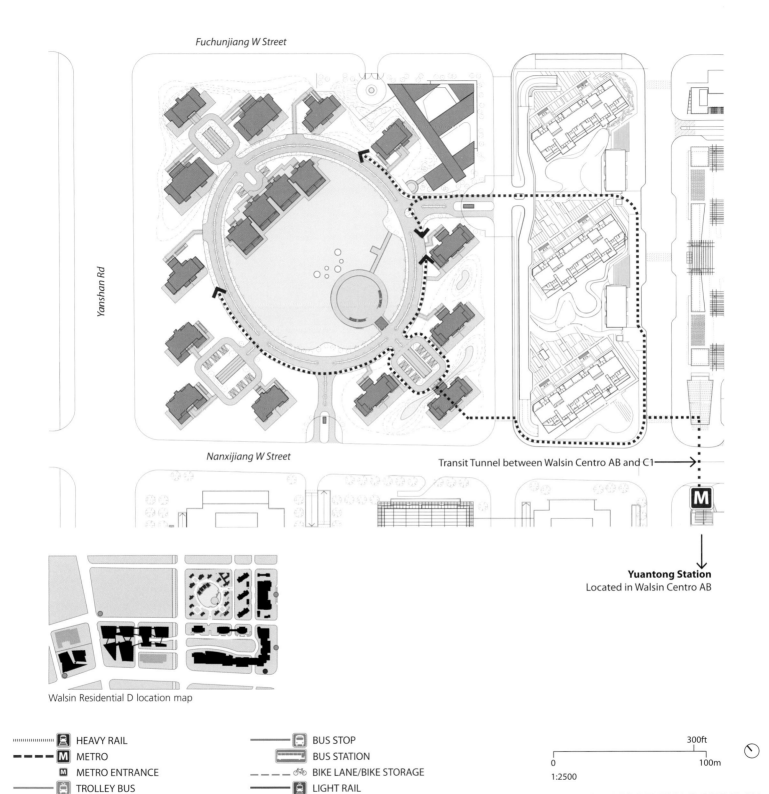

Fuchunjiang W Street

Yanshan Rd

Nanxijiang W Street

Transit Tunnel between Walsin Centro AB and C1 ⟶

Yuantong Station
Located in Walsin Centro AB

Walsin Residential D location map

	HEAVY RAIL			BUS STOP
	METRO			BUS STATION
	METRO ENTRANCE			BIKE LANE/BIKE STORAGE
	TROLLEY BUS			LIGHT RAIL
	TAXI STAND			TRANSIT/PEDESTRIAN LINKAGES

300ft

0   100m

1:2500

WALSIN RESIDENTIAL D SITE PLAN

Nanjing Taiwan Trade Mart

Public Sector Needs

When the City of Nanjing approached the developer of the Walsin Centro AB and Walsin Village & Residential projects regarding the development of the first business-to-business trade complex to encourage cross-Strait commercial trade between China and Taiwan, only three months were allotted to design the project and break ground, and six months to construct and complete shop fit out for the 328,084-square-foot (100,000-square-meter), ten-building complex. The project, located in a transit station environment about half a kilometer from the subway station, required relatively few parking spaces due to it being a "business-to-business" enterprise.

Private Sector Needs

The developer required the City of Nanjing to embrace a design solution that could be conceived and thoroughly developed working through the American end-of-year and Chinese lunar New Year holidays. Further, the project needed to be rapidly constructed, and meet all city planning and building code requirements. Finally, they needed the city planning officials to agree that significantly fewer than normal parking spaces could satisfy the code demand as an additional result of transit station proximity.

Project Issues

The project would occupy two sites on a prominent avenue, separated by a local street. The acute geometry of the two adjoining blocks created unusual planning opportunities. As the subway line ran under a corner of the site, near the street intersection, nothing could be built over the submerged right of way. Further, an open-air canal separated the Nanjing Taiwan Trade Mart site from the adjacent Walsin Centro AB site.

Solutions

To satisfy the transit environment design issues, ease of pedestrian access needed to be assured between Nanjing Taiwan Trade Mart and the Walsin Centro AB development, which separated and connected it to the Yuan Tong metro station. That access is provided centrally, linking the heart of the two-level, open-air Trade Mart mall to the grand park around which the retail center, hotel, and four office towers sit. Bus stops are located directly adjacent to the project boundary. Additionally, accommodation for a much reduced parking space count was negotiated with the city as a consequence of being in a transit environment.

Public Benefits

Beyond the obvious benefits of encouraging the use of public transit, both subway and bus, the reduction of parking for personal vehicles has additional environmental benefits.

Two-level open air trade mart

Bridge connection

Aerial view

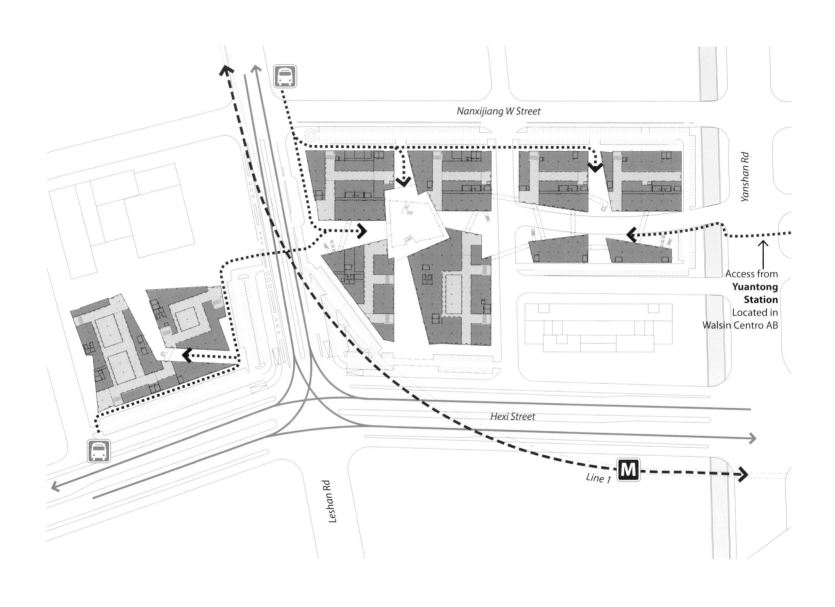

Nanxijiang W Street

Yanshan Rd

Access from
**Yuantong
Station**
Located in
Walsin Centro AB

Hexi Street

Leshan Rd

Line 1 M

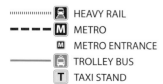

	HEAVY RAIL
	M METRO
	M METRO ENTRANCE
	TROLLEY BUS
	T TAXI STAND

	BUS STOP
	BUS STATION
	BIKE LANE/BIKE STORAGE
	LIGHT RAIL
	TRANSIT/PEDESTRIAN LINKAGES

150ft

0   50m
1:3500

NANJING TAIWAN TRADE MART SITE PLAN

Upper level shops

Nanjing Taiwan Trade Mart location map

Building colors and signage

TRANSIT STATION DESIGN

Transit Station Design

Far more than simple portals connecting transit systems to their local stops, transit stations must serve the multiple functional needs of all their constituencies including passengers, transit authorities, governing bodies and, with increasing frequency, private sector businesses. At the same time, the stations are part of the image of the agency and government to the riders and can serve an aspirational role for the community.

Functionally, the design of the transit station should facilitate the movement of the passengers from the outside world through the station to the transit vehicles. Program, schedule and budget are but the point of departure. Ease of access, egress and navigation are critical, particularly in complex multi-modal environments. Durability and serviceability count for cost-conscious agencies, while passengers want a sense of orientation, order and, if possible, a sense of place.

Great transit station design has the potential to deliver more at every level, and when it does it transforms the experience, increasing ridership, building loyalty and creating commercial opportunity. Entrances, concourses, platforms, lighting, signage, form and color are all part of the customer experience and can be leveraged to benefit all.

Sengkang MRT Station
Singapore

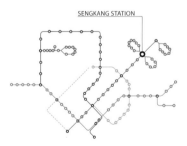

Singapore MRT and LRT

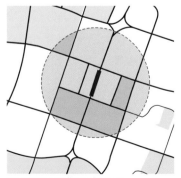

15-minute walking distance

Public Sector Needs

The Singapore Land Transport Authority (LTA) established the Northeast Line (NEL) to help address long-term housing, educational and employment issues, as population densities in central Singapore have become less sustainable over time. The line links to planned centers of living that will grow into self-sustaining districts. As one of 12 stations along the new line, Sengkang Station is one component of a new transportation system that embodies Singapore's commitment to world-class infrastructure.

Private Sector Needs

As the station site, a full four blocks in expanse, is planned as the center of the town of Sengkang, the public sector needed to leverage connectivity to the large numbers of commuters entering and exiting the LRT, rail, bus and taxi stand as well as pedestrian bridges daily. Visibility, accessibility and ease of navigation at the station serve the adjacent development.

Project Issues

The multi-modal station has a distinctly urban character that is defined by its location at the juncture of a master planned district that includes mixed-use development, a bus depot, taxi station, the regional, light rail system above-ground, and the MRT subway below. Critical access through and around the station was necessary at both the ground level and the mezzanine level.

Design Solutions

Simplicity of form and clarity of organization facilitate the movement of passengers between the various functions of the station, the transit system and the adjacent office and residential development. Dual sets of up and down escalators maximize views and speed pedestrian traffic, whether passengers are traveling in and out or changing modes of transit at Sengkang.

Visual connections to the sun and sky are reinforced throughout all levels of the project. A sweeping, oval-shaped canopy shields the roof-level platforms of the light rail system, while large expanses of glass allow light to flow down to the mezzanine and subway platforms. The oval shape of the station envelope eliminates corners, and encourages

Vertical transport system

pedestrian flows into and out of as well as around the station environment. Entrances and pedestrian bridges, covered with a Teflon-coated fabric, establish a distinctive image for the transportation system even as it provides protection from the sun and the brief tropical showers that occur throughout the region.

Public Benefits

Sengkang Station provides a convenient multi-modal transit center for a growing urban district. Both high profile and highly functional, the station provides an anchor for Sengkang's development and a gateway to Singapore and the region.

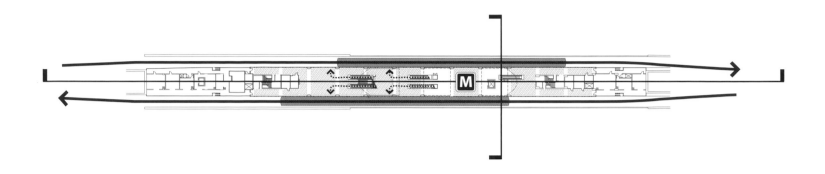

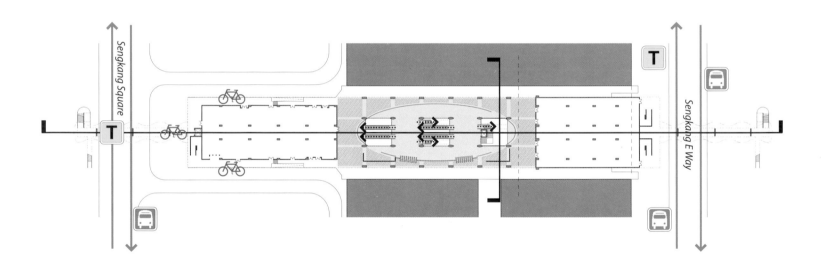

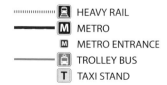

HEAVY RAIL
METRO
METRO ENTRANCE
TROLLEY BUS
TAXI STAND

BUS STOP
BUS STATION
BIKE LANE/BIKE STORAGE
LIGHT RAIL
TRANSIT/PEDESTRIAN LINKAGES

150ft

0   50m
1:1500

SENGKANG STATION SUBWAY
AND GROUND LEVEL/CONCOURSE LEVELS

Grand hall

MRT boarding area

MRT platform level

LRT platform level

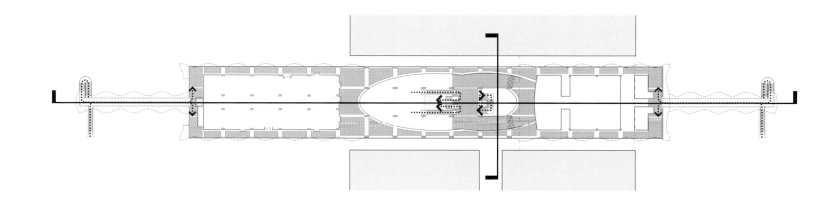

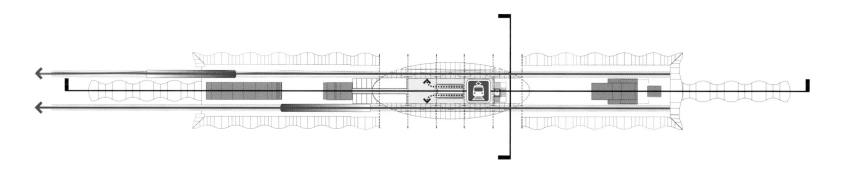

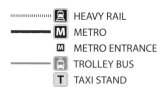

- ▥ HEAVY RAIL
- Ⓜ METRO
- Ⓜ METRO ENTRANCE
- ▥ TROLLEY BUS
- Ⓣ TAXI STAND

- ▣ BUS STOP
- ▤ BUS STATION
- ⊘ BIKE LANE/BIKE STORAGE
- ▣ LIGHT RAIL
- ⋯⋯▶ TRANSIT/PEDESTRIAN LINKAGES

150ft

0   50m
1:1500

SENGKANG STATION MEZZANINE
AND PLATFORM LEVELS

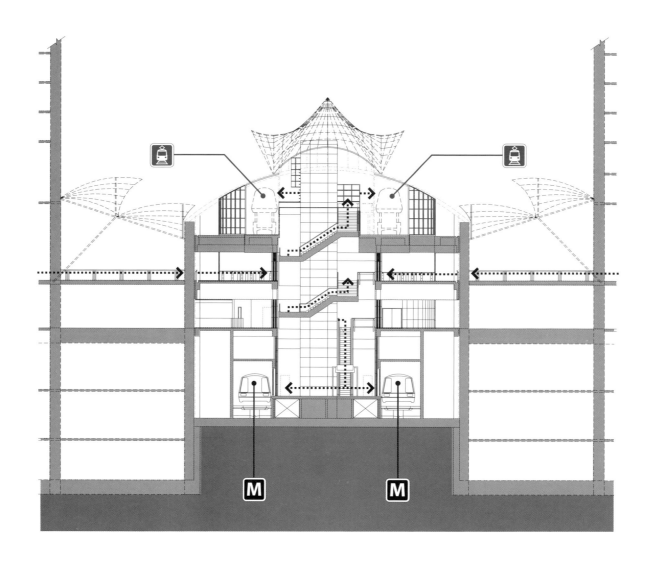

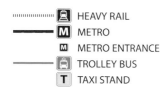

HEAVY RAIL	
METRO	
METRO ENTRANCE	
TROLLEY BUS	
TAXI STAND	

BUS STOP	
BUS STATION	
BIKE LANE/BIKE STORAGE	
LIGHT RAIL	
TRANSIT/PEDESTRIAN LINKAGES	

SENGKANG STATION CROSS SECTION

Public lobby

Public lobby

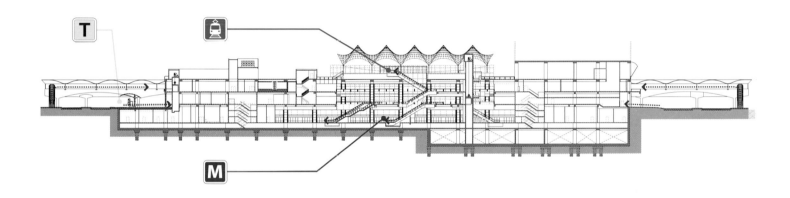

150ft

0

1:1500

50m

SENGKANG STATION LONGITUDINAL SECTION

Buangkok MRT Station
Singapore

Singapore MRT and LRT

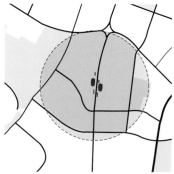

15-minute walking distance

Public Sector Needs
Also situated on the Northeast Line (NEL), Buangkok Station is a linear, mid-line, suburban station located in a largely high-rise and high-density residential district of Buangkok, just one stop from Sengkang Station, which intersects the subway and local bus service with a master planned residential community.

Private Sector Needs
Private sector requirements were primarily future focused as it was anticipated that the area around the station would grow into a busy commercial center over time. It was important to provide adequate room and clear pathways for the street crossing through the mezzanine, an effective location for the kiss 'n' ride drop-off, and both bus and taxi transfer. In addition, there was a current need for transit-related retail at the station.

Project Issues
To conform with Singapore's active civil defense program, there was a requirement for the mezzanine and below-ground platform levels of Buangkok to provide shelter to citizens in the event of a major catastrophic event. The design needed to integrate blast doors, blast reduction blind corners, and sanitary and living facilities without degrading passenger flows or the look, feel and presence of the state-of-the-art transit facility. At ground level the site was bifurcated by a divided roadway.

Design Solutions
While the civil defense program required the segregation of the station interiors from the exterior, the use of gracious ceiling forms and light colors and materials celebrate the spirit of Singapore. The idea of a big Singapore sky is represented in the central platform and surrounding mezzanine levels with a gentle vault in the station interior ceiling. The use of glass and stainless steel railings around the mezzanine allows a very open experience and a high degree of visibility in a very compact interior space.

The above-ground portions of the station straddle the divided road with two structures that provide for taxi, bus and kiss 'n' ride pick-up and drop-off. The interlinked steel structures, covered in tensile Teflon-coated fiberglass cover all major transit components and provide protection from tropical rain, sun, heat and ultraviolet light.

Station exterior

Taxi, bus and kiss 'n' ride pick-up and drop-off

The fabric roofs allow for significant natural light to penetrate the station area, as well as the retail and below-ground station area stair access. The fabric structures, lit from the steel structure below, bounce light down and create a glowing presence visible to the adjacent residential development.

Public Benefits

The station creates a day and night icon and anchor for the burgeoning new town. At the same time, it offers effective protection for passengers from the equatorial climate with the first use of Teflon-coated fiberglass for transit in Singapore. Finally, it serves as a key component of the civil defense program.

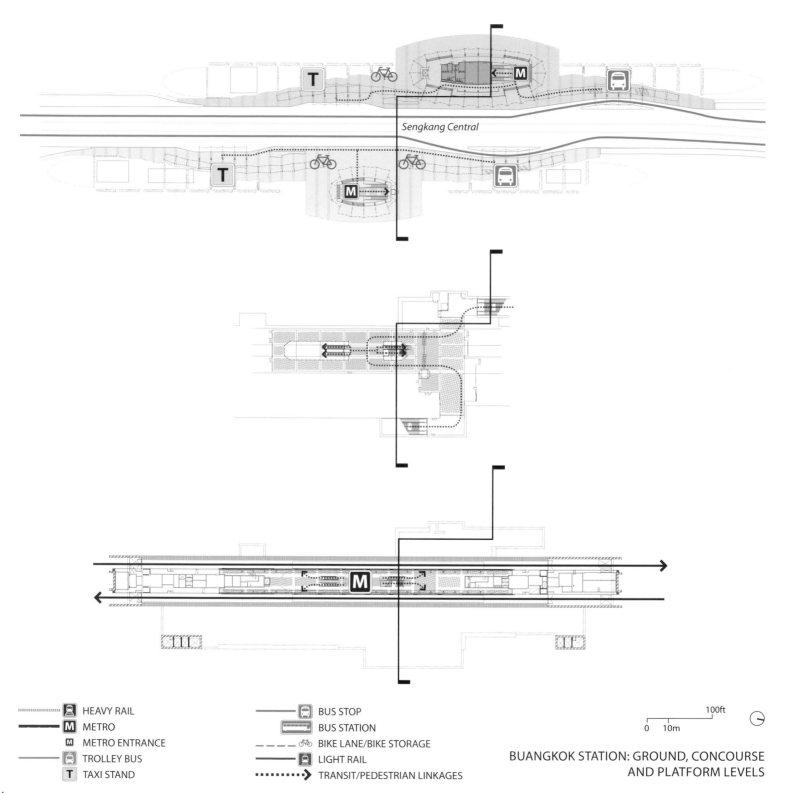

Sengkang Central

HEAVY RAIL
METRO
METRO ENTRANCE
TROLLEY BUS
T TAXI STAND

BUS STOP
BUS STATION
BIKE LANE/BIKE STORAGE
LIGHT RAIL
TRANSIT/PEDESTRIAN LINKAGES

100ft
0   10m

BUANGKOK STATION: GROUND, CONCOURSE
AND PLATFORM LEVELS

Concourse level

MRT boarding area

MRT platform level

Steel structure/Tensile fiberglass

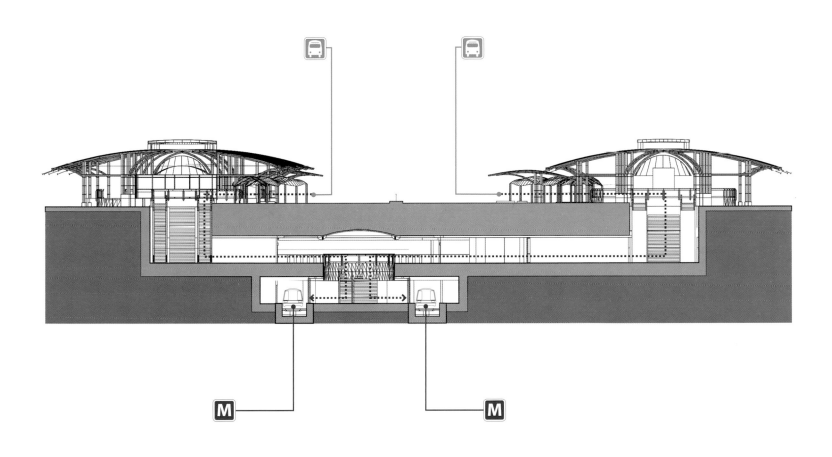

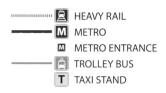

HEAVY RAIL

M METRO

M METRO ENTRANCE

TROLLEY BUS

T TAXI STAND

BUS STOP

BUS STATION

BIKE LANE/BIKE STORAGE

LIGHT RAIL

TRANSIT/PEDESTRIAN LINKAGES

50ft

0   5m

BUANGKOK STATION: CROSS SECTION

Pico/San Vicente Station

Los Angeles, California

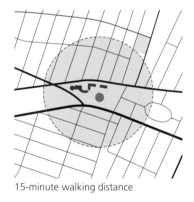

15-minute walking distance

Public Sector Needs

The station site at Pico and San Vicente was identified as part of a plan to extend the fledgling subway west toward the Pacific. The site had long provided an on-grade bus transfer terminal between the Rapid Transit District (RTD) and Santa Monica Bus Lines. Additionally, both Pico Boulevard and Venice Boulevard were major east–west commercial strips that were beginning to enjoy a renaissance. During the study for joint development opportunities, a light rail component was added to the site program that would potentially link the bus terminal and the subway Red Line with an at-grade or elevated light rail that would extend to Los Angeles International Airport. At the same time, the site was large enough and had sufficient regional street access to easily accommodate complementary commercial and community uses. With careful coupling of the transit components, a mixed-use project with retail, office, community uses, shared parking along with hotel, residential and/or office, the transit uses could be concealed from the direct view of adjacent residential above Venice Boulevard.

Private Sector Needs

From the private development perspective, access from all three major streets—with positive flow traffic and potential customers for a mix of uses—would be of value. It would be important to ensure that each proposed use could meet particular requirements without compromising any of the parts or the project as a whole.

Project Issues

The triangular site with two-sided access posed challenges for placing vehicular ingress and egress points so as not to disrupt street continuity. Further, the slope of the parcel created major grade changes.

Design Solutions

The proposed design capitalized on the major grade changes between Venice Boulevard and W Pico Boulevard to tuck the bus transfer terminal off the Pico frontage, against the light rail platform and the Venice Boulevard retaining edge. The careful layering of trays of space and use allowed for more than one pedestrian level on the street and protected the single side access to the station. On Pico Boulevard the ground level would be lower, facing the neighborhood to the north, while on Venice Boulevard the upper ground level would face south. The plan allowed for uses on two levels, each with an easy pedestrian flow from street front to the transit options within the site. For future planning, the design anticipated the placement of the planned light rail to and from the airport behind the bus station, as well as the accommodation of the proposed Red Line subway below. The upper levels could be stacked mixed-use development including retail, office and residential.

Public Benefits

The design of the station site creates a major multi-modal hub in a major inner city neighborhood area. By placing all of the transit components below and behind the façades of commercial, retail, entertainment and residential, the station has a neighborhood-friendly face, which also mitigates noise and other nuisances generated by the transit.

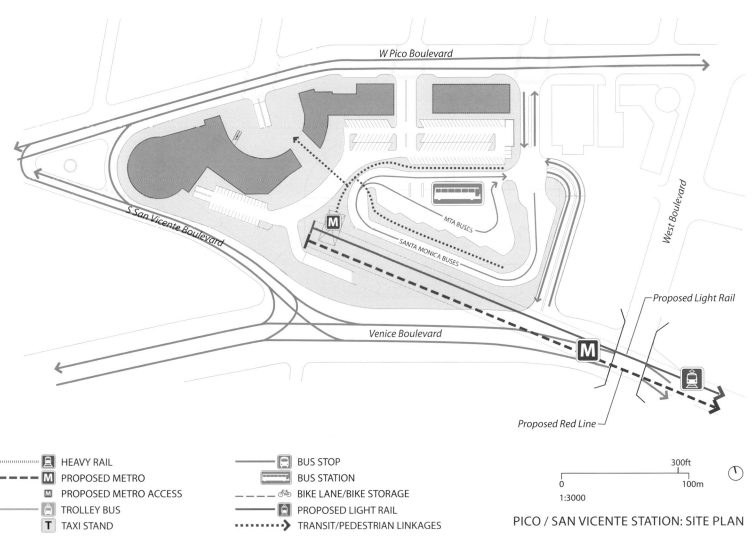

	HEAVY RAIL		BUS STOP
M	PROPOSED METRO		BUS STATION
M	PROPOSED METRO ACCESS		BIKE LANE/BIKE STORAGE
	TROLLEY BUS		PROPOSED LIGHT RAIL
T	TAXI STAND		TRANSIT/PEDESTRIAN LINKAGES

300ft
0   100m
1:3000

PICO / SAN VICENTE STATION: SITE PLAN

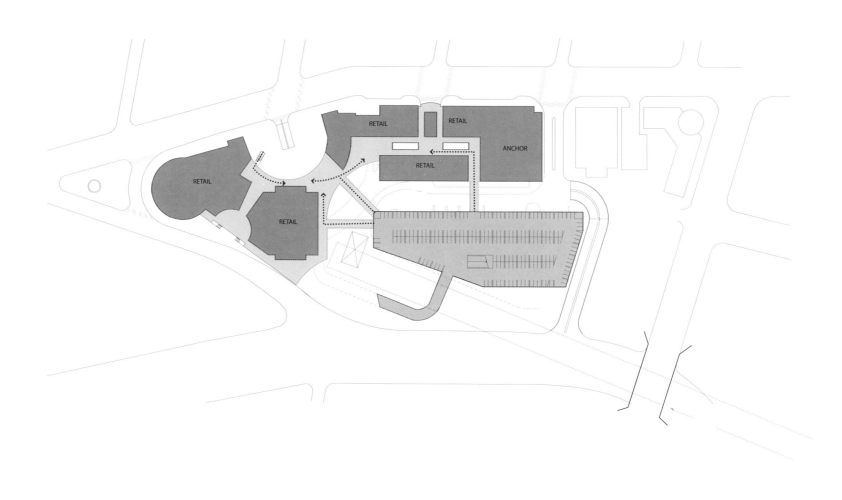

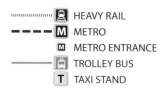

HEAVY RAIL

METRO

METRO ENTRANCE

TROLLEY BUS

TAXI STAND

BUS STOP

BUS STATION

BIKE LANE/BIKE STORAGE

LIGHT RAIL

TRANSIT/PEDESTRIAN LINKAGES

300ft

0   100m

1:3000

PICO / SAN VICENTE STATION: LEVEL 2

RETAIL

RETAIL

RETAIL

RETAIL

ANCHOR

RETAIL

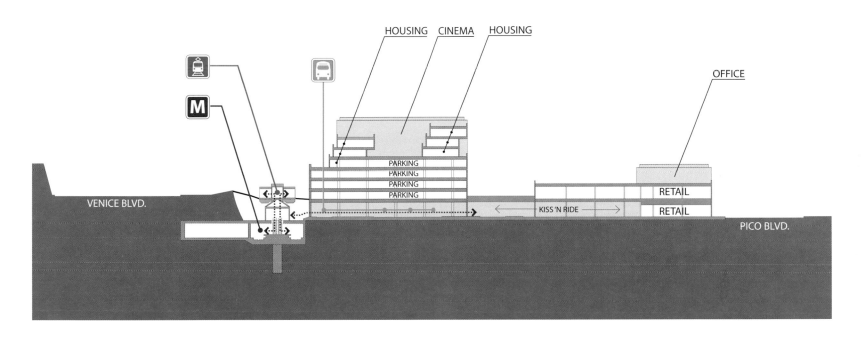

HOUSING   CINEMA   HOUSING

OFFICE

VENICE BLVD.

PARKING
PARKING
PARKING
PARKING

KISS 'N RIDE

RETAIL

RETAIL

PICO BLVD.

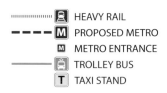

HEAVY RAIL
PROPOSED METRO
METRO ENTRANCE
TROLLEY BUS
TAXI STAND

BUS STOP
BUS STATION
BIKE LANE/BIKE STORAGE
PROPOSED LIGHT RAIL
TRANSIT/PEDESTRIAN LINKAGES

150ft

0   50m

1:1250

PICO / SAN VICENTE STATION: SECTION

TRANSIT STATION DESIGN   51

TRANSIT ORIENTED DEVELOPMENT

Transit Oriented Development

A Transit Oriented Development (TOD), as used in the context of this book, is a real estate project developed above and/or immediately adjacent to existing or planned underground or surface public transit rail or fixed path lines, providing direct access to the transit station. This access may be located below grade at a concourse level or at grade emerging from a station below. However, passengers or pedestrians must not have to cross traffic to access the development.

The examples collected here were designed in cooperation with the responsible public agencies to ensure connection to the station boxes satisfied the requirements for customer flow as well as the development's need for linkage to the transit stations. In all cases, existing transit lines—including high-speed train, passenger rail, light rail, subway, bus and taxi stands—were operational or in construction at the time of the development. The construction that occurred above the transit stations responded to the functional, environmental, and emergency needs of the transit stations, and provided the separation necessary to accommodate vibration and noise. At the same time, the designs ensure the convenient conversion of passenger traffic into customer traffic as passengers exit the transit realm and enter the commercial venue.

The designed and built examples depicted here are located in Asia, Eastern and Central Europe, Canada and the United States.

Kowloon Station
Hong Kong

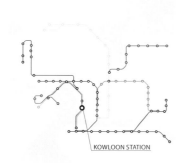

KOWLOON STATION

Hong Kong subway and rail

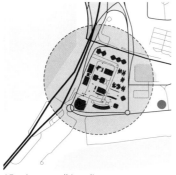

15-minute walking distance

Public Sector Needs

The MTR (Mass Transit Railway) Corporation saw the construction of the new Hong Kong Airport as a catalyst with the potential to significantly transform the entire public transit system serving Hong Kong, Kowloon, and the New Territories. The construction of transit-oriented, mixed-use developments above each station would not only provide for multiple uses on each piece of precious land, but also create a destination in each location that in turn would stimulate increased ridership on the already well-utilized subway and bus lines, and contribute to the reduction of personal vehicle traffic. The goal was to create world-class destinations with world-class buildings, featuring state-of-the-art, functional design.

Transportation issues, which had been adequately addressed by the transit planners, included the careful confluence of logistics and transit geometries among the high-speed airport train, subway, long haul and regional bus stations, local buses, and a large, fluid, taxi queue.

Private Sector Needs

From a development perspective, it was essential to create a minimally compromised, flexible, efficient, well-functioning retail center with natural light. Further, the center required direct access to the transit station, all modes of transportation, as well as each of the towers, to be located above. Finally, it was important to provide a clear identity, positive image, and pedestrian access to neighboring blocks. Servicing for the retail functions needed to be as direct as possible.

Project Issues

With structural and building systems impeding the retail program from below and above, the challenges were daunting. Critical issues revolved around the constraints of working above an active multi-modal transit station, with limitations on the locations of column footings for the new buildings, and the imposition of numerous transit line blast shafts, elevator cores, escalators, and exit stairways, all of which needed to penetrate the commercial retail floors up through to the podium. Additionally, the numerous residential towers, office buildings and potential hotel buildings required independent structures and foundations, separate servicing, and individual fire/life safety systems. The podium deck, with accommodation for private and emergency vehicle access, further complicated the planning and design process.

Aerial perspective

Design Solutions

The design concept and schematic design created a fluid path for customer flow. With frequent podium deck penetrations to bathe the mall with natural light, and with openings in the floor to allow light to pass through to the lower level, a customer-friendly navigational path became a natural extension of the transit journey. Grand, multi-level entry structures provide sunlit spaces for gathering, while announcing the rich retail offering to the streets surrounding the project.

Public Benefits

The project serves as the first and largest point of entry to Hong Kong from the international airport, as well as a dispersion hub to serve local and regional communities. The civic spaces—both on the podium deck and within the project—and the wide range of dining, entertainment and retail options, create a sense of destination, which fulfills the programmatic mandate on every level.

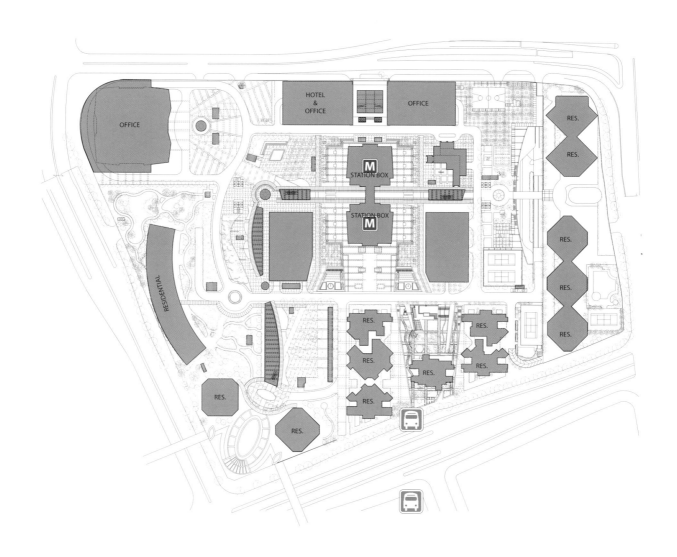

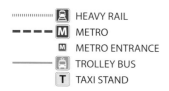

HEAVY RAIL

METRO

METRO ENTRANCE

TROLLEY BUS

TAXI STAND

BUS STOP

BUS STATION

BIKE LANE/BIKE STORAGE

LIGHT RAIL

TRANSIT/PEDESTRIAN LINKAGES

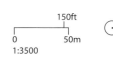

150ft

0   50m

1:3500

KOWLOON STATION ROOF PLAN

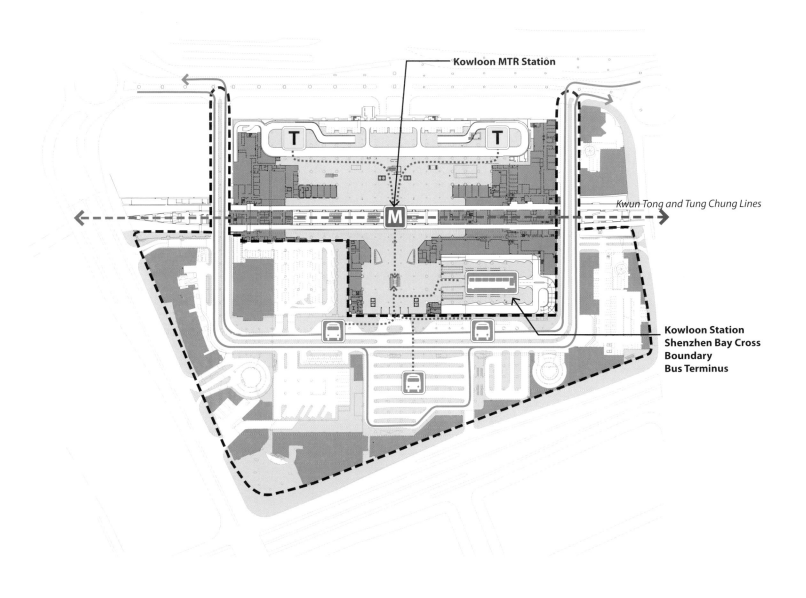

Kowloon MTR Station

T   T

Kwun Tong and Tung Chung Lines

Kowloon Station Shenzhen Bay Cross Boundary Bus Terminus

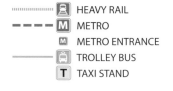

HEAVY RAIL		
METRO		
METRO ENTRANCE		
TROLLEY BUS		
TAXI STAND		

BUS STOP
BUS STATION
BIKE LANE/BIKE STORAGE
LIGHT RAIL
TRANSIT/PEDESTRIAN LINKAGES

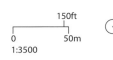

150ft

0   50m
1:3500

KOWLOON STATION COMPOSITE SITE PLAN

TRANSIT ORIENTED DEVELOPMENT   57

Transit station ticket concourse

Podium/retail linkage

Podium level civic space

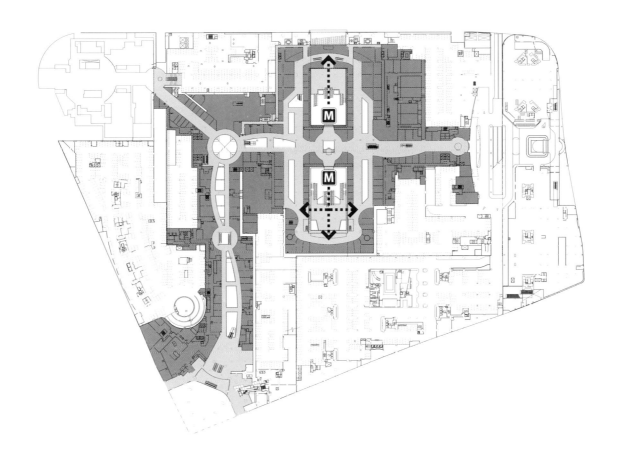

	HEAVY RAIL		BUS STOP
	METRO		BUS STATION
	METRO ENTRANCE		BIKE LANE/BIKE STORAGE
	TROLLEY BUS		LIGHT RAIL
	TAXI STAND		TRANSIT/PEDESTRIAN LINKAGES

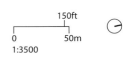

150ft
0   50m
1:3500

KOWLOON STATION LEVEL 2

Hollywood & Highland

Los Angeles, California

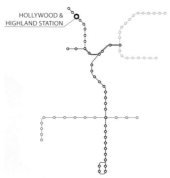

Los Angeles Metro

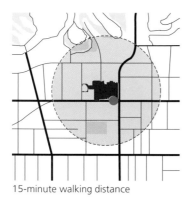

15-minute walking distance

Public Sector Needs

Metro, the Los Angeles County Metropolitan Transit Authority, had begun the initial line of a larger plan for the subway system. The several surface light rail lines in place were functioning well. The goal was to have stations located at existing destinations, or where they might be built. As part of the Red Line Metro, a subway station was planned at the western end of Hollywood Boulevard, at the intersection of Highland Avenue, half a mile south of the Hollywood Bowl. The site is adjacent to the famous Grauman's Chinese Theater, renowned for the hand and footprints of movie stars in its concrete forecourt. Knowing that a major mixed-use retail/hotel/entertainment complex was being planned for the site directly above the station, Metro envisioned a world-class destination that would attract ridership; and they saw the opportunity for a park 'n' ride facility in the basement of the new project, which would conveniently feed customers to the subway.

Private Sector Needs

The owner, retail developer TrizecHahn, wanted a strong draw for both tourists and residents. They envisioned the Kodak Theatre hosting the annual Academy Awards presentation—a goal now realized. To accommodate the requirement, a grand ballroom and cinema became part of the program, with project imagery inspired by the legendary Hollywood era of silent movies. Linkage to the Chinese Theater and the powerful draw of Hollywood Boulevard was also a compelling argument for development.

Project Issues

Building on a constrained, urban site directly above a transit station posed challenges, including construction logistics, vibration, structural isolation, blast shafts and exiting. The out of sequence placement of 7-foot-deep (2.1 meters) steel structural beams spanning the station box, and the prohibition of using heavy equipment over the station created additional construction complications and costs. The complex servicing challenges of a live theater, ballroom, hotel/conference center, and retail/dining project—all above a transit line and station—were daunting.

Hollywood & Highland/Hollywood Boulevard context

Design Solutions

Hollywood & Highland is designed to engage pedestrians on the street, while integrating with public transit. The Metro portal, located on the façade of the complex, feeds directly to the sidewalk on Hollywood Boulevard. A short walk west takes visitors to the major entrance of the open-air, multi-level grand courtyard of the complex, surrounded by retail shops and restaurants, with direct access to the hotel, cinema, Kodak Theatre and grand ballroom. Street-facing shops open onto the forecourt of the Chinese Theater and the "Walk of Fame" along Hollywood Boulevard. Bus stops on both streets also bring visitors to this site.

Public Benefits

The resulting project is a tourist and cultural destination. People arrive by subway and bus to visit the retail offerings, cafes and restaurants, cultural and entertainment venues, cinema, and the Chinese Theater. The adjacent hotel is conveniently served by rapid transit. In addition, with Hollywood & Vine on the eastern end of the boulevard, and Hollywood & Highland on the western end—both served by Metro subway stations—the historic one-mile commercial stretch is enjoying a redevelopment renaissance.

Street-facing shops and Metro portal

Metro portal

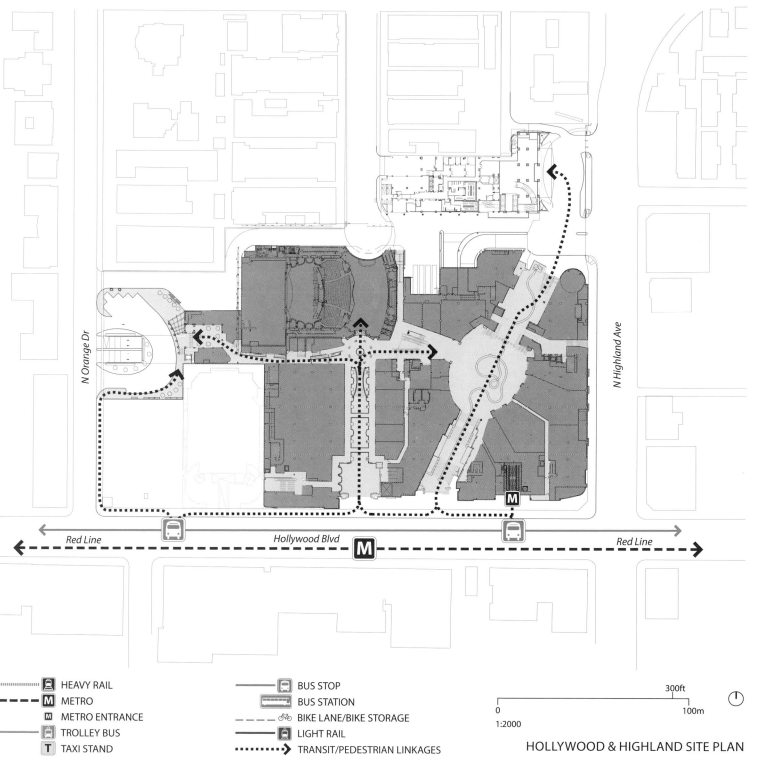

N Orange Dr

N Highland Ave

Red Line   Hollywood Blvd   **M**   Red Line

HEAVY RAIL
M METRO
M METRO ENTRANCE
TROLLEY BUS
T TAXI STAND
BUS STOP
BUS STATION
BIKE LANE/BIKE STORAGE
LIGHT RAIL
TRANSIT/PEDESTRIAN LINKAGES

300ft

0   100m

1:2000

HOLLYWOOD & HIGHLAND SITE PLAN

Toronto Union Station

Toronto, Ontario, Canada

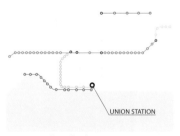

Toronto rail and subway

15-minute walking distance

Public Sector Needs

Union Station is a revered historic structure linking the heart of downtown Toronto with regional suburbs, as well as national and U.S. cities. A multi-modal hub, it integrates Via Rail Canada, GO Transit, the TTC subway trains, a major bus transfer station, and is scheduled to accommodate the Air Train connection to Toronto International Airport. Furthermore, it links directly to the Path, a multi-mile system of underground retail concourses that provide all-weather connections between numerous blocks of the downtown business and cultural districts.

Having envisioned a massive "dig down" to provide for retail activity underneath the heavy rail tracks and some existing buildings, the City of Toronto sought a retail development strategy which would not interfere with the separate multi-modal station operations or the 65 million passengers who would circulate through the project every year, and would respect the historic structure above. Finally, Parks Canada, the historic preservation authority, needed to approve any refurbishment to the existing facilities and all new construction for aesthetic compatibility.

Private Sector Needs

Redcliff Realty Advisors, the head lease developer responsible for the implementation of a bold new vision, needed the retail concourses to operate with minimal interference from the demands of the transit components overhead, while taking advantage of their proximity. In spite of the imposition of the structures necessary to support heavy rail trains above, and the logistical challenges of servicing retail shops and dining facilities, the additional retail area needed to operate efficiently, with the critical mass to create a sense of destination and attract the widest possible spectrum of customers.

Project Issues

Located between the two busiest north–south avenues in the financial district of Toronto, Union Station sits in the midst of the convention center, the CN Tower, the Air Canada Center—home to the Toronto Maple Leafs NHL hockey and Toronto Raptors NBA basketball teams—and is close to the Toronto Blue Jays American League baseball stadium, the historic St. Lawrence Market, and the Sony Centre and Four Seasons Centre Performing Arts complexes. The new retail concourse would be constructed under some portions of a historic

Retail concourse (Rendering image courtesy of NORR Limited, Prime Design Architect and Engineers)

building as well as beneath two operating railroad systems. At the same time, the design had to accommodate plans for the Air Tran, which would be constructed above the concourse. Approval from Parks Canada was required, but not assured.

Design Solutions

The design concept transforms the existing facility, whose primary purpose had been to move passengers efficiently through the station, into a nexus of destinations enticing people to meet, dine, shop, and mingle—a "destination of destinations" in the heart of the city, serving as a pivotal point for all the exceptional activities that surround it.

Public Benefits

The strategy informing the project was based on a merchandising concept that creates a collection of destinations, each fulfilling the unmet needs of transit customers, tourists, office workers and residents. As the first point of arrival on the way to work, and the final point of departure on the way home, quality and convenience were central. Divided into zones designated for a fresh market, places to purchase prepared gourmet meals, fast foods, restaurants, travel-related merchandise, women's and men's fashion, stores tending to business needs, and "The Best of Canada", Union Station becomes a multi-modal transit portal offering a cornucopia of local foods and merchandise that attracts commuters, tourists and visitors.

GO Transit concourse

Historic West Wing
(Rendering images courtesy of NORR Limited, Prime Design Architect and Engineers)

DRYWALL CEILING
BY OWNER

METAL PANEL CEILING
BY OWNER

CONTINUOUS ALUMINUM
LOUVERS BY OWNER

CEILING MOUNTED
BLADE SIGN, MOUNTING
BRACKET & BLADE BY
LANDLORD. COPY BY
TENANT

SIGNAGE

0.77 m [2'-6"]

SIGNAGE ZONE
(0.3 m +/-)

INDIVIDUAL LETTER
SIGNAGE BY TENANT,
CENTERED ON STOREFRONT

3.35 m [11'-0"]
3.50 m [11'-6"]
3.80 m [12'-6"]

LIMESTONE
COLUMN
BY OWNER

ENTRY CENTERED ON
STOREFRONT
BY TENANT

6" BLACK ANODIZED ALUMINUM
FRAME ON ALUMINUM BASE
BY LANDLORD (0.152m)

BLACK ANODIZED ALUMINUM
BASE BY LANDLORD

STONE BASE
BY TENANT

GRANITE BASE
BY OWNER

Tenant design criteria standards

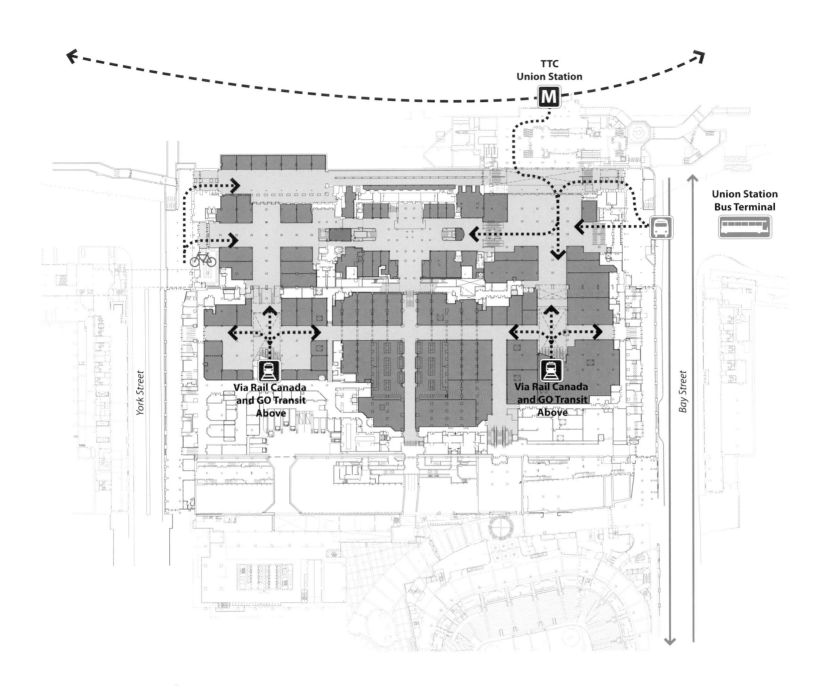

TTC
Union Station

Union Station
Bus Terminal

York Street

Bay Street

Via Rail Canada
and GO Transit
Above

Via Rail Canada
and GO Transit
Above

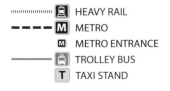

🚈 HEAVY RAIL

Ⓜ METRO

Ⓜ METRO ENTRANCE

🚋 TROLLEY BUS

Ⓣ TAXI STAND

🚌 BUS STOP

🚌 BUS STATION

🚲 BIKE LANE/BIKE STORAGE

🚈 LIGHT RAIL

TRANSIT/PEDESTRIAN LINKAGES

300ft

0   100m

1:2000

UNION STATION PROMENADE LEVEL PLAN

Centrum Chodov

Prague, Czech Republic

Prague metro

15-minute walking distance

Public Sector Needs

The urban growth patterns of Prague in the 1970s and 80s were such that new dwelling units were accommodated in Soviet-style towers located in satellite communities, accessible by regional road networks and, more importantly, a sophisticated mass transit system. The resulting land use included large undeveloped areas and isolated, anonymous housing blocks, detached from their context and with little sense of community. Prague had the transit infrastructure in place to create new, accessible urban development; however, the city needed private investors to fund projects around transit hubs.

Private Sector Needs

From a development standpoint, it was essential that the city and transport authorities support new district master plans embracing higher density and mixed-use projects, in line with market demand and land values. This would enable private developers to fund and fill projects worthy of Prague and its key location in Europe.

Project Issues

Critical project issues revolved around the design criteria, set by local authorities, regarding building next to and above the existing subway system, as well as how the project would link to the subway and bus networks. In addition, access to the site by service and private vehicles required significant coordination with both city and regional authorities.

Design Solutions

The 678,000-square-foot (63,000-square-meter) retail development forms the first phase of a vibrant new town center. The project fulfills a strong retail demand, while providing meaningful public spaces woven into the community. The multi-level, organic plan responds to the geographical context of the site, and its position on the seam between urban Prague and the surrounding countryside. The massing and materiality of the project evoke interplay between urban typologies and the scale and vistas inherent to the hillsides of greater Prague. Centrum Chodov also provides an appropriate response to Prague's highway, subway and bus infrastructure, with easy access for mass transit and private vehicles, multi-story car parks with a capacity of nearly 2400 parking spaces, and a subway station linking directly to the project.

Metro portal/Bus station

Metro linkage to retail

Public Benefits

This and other projects realized within the master plan provide the
community with a wide variety of new retail, dining, entertainment, and
living and working opportunities, as well as new civic spaces, plazas,
and connectivity to Prague's transit networks. Public benefits include the
realization of a sustainable urban development that sets the groundwork
for future phases that will further enrich the diversity of the urban fabric.
Prague has one of the best public transportation systems in Europe—the
metro, trams and buses are used by two-thirds of Prague's population, and
cover the majority of the city and outskirts. Centrum Chodov serves as an
important amenity for Prague's transit network.

Interior vertical circulation

Interior mall

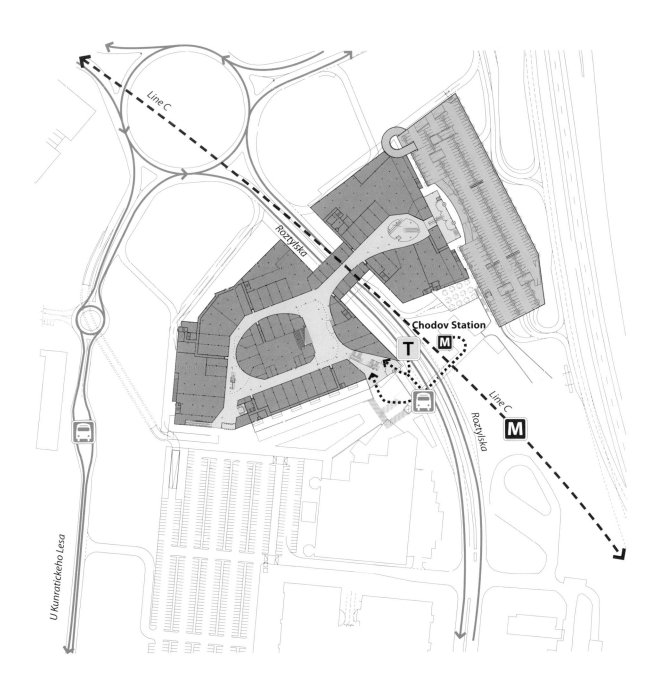

Chodov Station

Line C

Roztylska

Line C

Roztylska

U Kunratickeho Lesa

HEAVY RAIL

METRO

METRO ENTRANCE

TROLLEY BUS

TAXI STAND

BUS STOP

BUS STATION

BIKE LANE/BIKE STORAGE

LIGHT RAIL

TRANSIT/PEDESTRIAN LINKAGES

300ft

0   100m

1:3000

CENTRUM CHODOV SITE PLAN

Metallist City Centre

Kharkiv, Ukraine

Kharkiv metro and rail

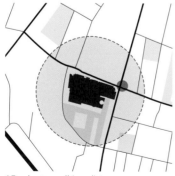

15-minute walking distance

Public Sector Needs

Metallist City Centre sits directly across the street from the Kharkiv Football Stadium, which is slated to host the UEFA Euro 2012 Finals for the next Federation Internationale de Football Association (FIFA) World Cup. Public transit—subway, light rail and bus lines—serves the shared intersection. Aware of weekend traffic impacts, the city planning and transit agencies sought a project that would recognize and embrace public transit as a primary means of engagement with the public, while mitigating the increase in traffic on days when games at the stadium boosted activity in the district.

Private Sector Needs

CD Capital Partners and CDCH, faced with significant planning and zoning restrictions imposed on the site due to its adjacency to a public school, sought a responsive site plan that responded to the context while linking directly to the subway. Given the complexities imposed by zoning regulations, they needed to maximize available project area and reduce costs. As the project was well served by the transit system, normal parking ratios could be minimized.

Project Issues

Planning for the urban site was fraught with the constraints of vehicular access/egress and servicing, and by height limits and mandatory setbacks. The building code offered the opportunity for parking above grade (with restrictions) and underneath the retail center as well. The subway tunnels, crossing beneath the primary corner of the site, needed to be bridged by a long span structure in order to create a landmark entry at the intersection. Structural isolation was required to remove vibration and noise transfer. Frequent delivery of merchandise also required significant on-site truck stacking to limit street congestion and interference with public transit.

Design Solutions

The concept was built around creating direct underground and at-grade linkages to the subway station. The light rail and bus stop locations were adjusted to provide convenient access to the project. Additionally, visitors to the stadium can utilize an under-street passage to access the retail center, and then move on to the subway station without having to go outdoors. The two primary entrances allow neighboring communities to use the retail galleria as a long block passage to the subway in severe temperatures.

Aerial view

Public Benefits

As envisioned, the mixed-use hotel/retail/entertainment complex encourages use of the existing public transit systems, thus reducing dependency on personal vehicles. By coupling the sporting venue with retail and dining opportunities, a more potent destination was created, and one which was readily accessible by three modes of public transit.

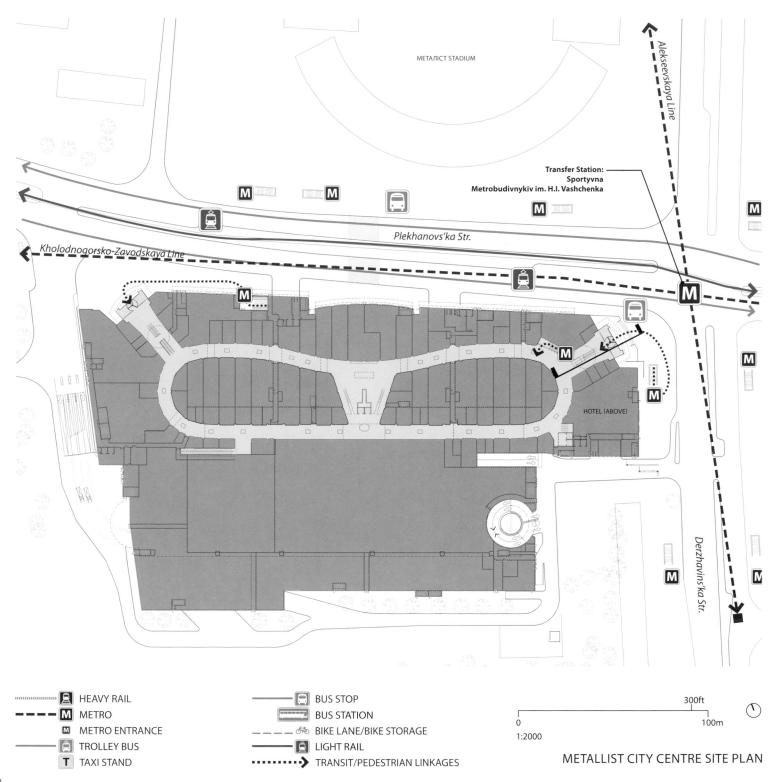

МЕТАЛІСТ STADIUM

Alekseevskaya Line

M ▨   M ▨   🚌   M ▨   M ▨

🚆

Transfer Station:
Sportyvna
Metrobudivnykiv im. H.I. Vashchenka

Plekhanovs'ka Str.

Kholodnogorsko-Zavodskaya Line

🚆

M

M

🚌

M

M

M

HOTEL (ABOVE)

M

Derzhavins'ka Str.

M   M

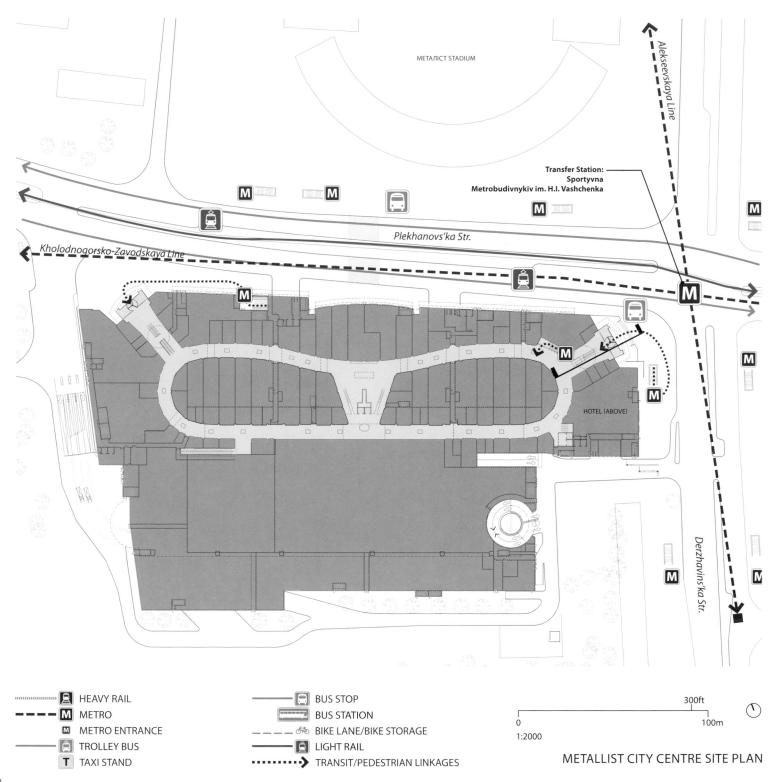

▦🚆	HEAVY RAIL		🚌	BUS STOP
▪▪▪M	METRO		🚍	BUS STATION
M	METRO ENTRANCE		🚲	BIKE LANE/BIKE STORAGE
🚎	TROLLEY BUS		🚈	LIGHT RAIL
T	TAXI STAND		▪▪▪▶	TRANSIT/PEDESTRIAN LINKAGES

300ft

0   100m

1:2000

METALLIST CITY CENTRE SITE PLAN

Central atrium

Retail galleria

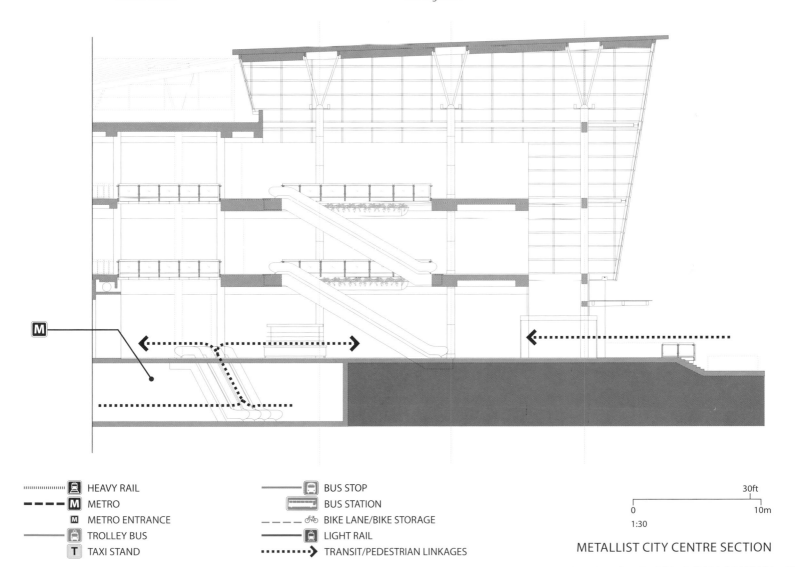

Ⓜ

▥ HEAVY RAIL		🚌 BUS STOP	
Ⓜ METRO		🚏 BUS STATION	
Ⓜ METRO ENTRANCE		🚲 BIKE LANE/BIKE STORAGE	
🚎 TROLLEY BUS		🚈 LIGHT RAIL	
T TAXI STAND		▸ TRANSIT/PEDESTRIAN LINKAGES	

0 ——— 30ft / 10m

1:30

Moskva Collection

Moscow, Russia

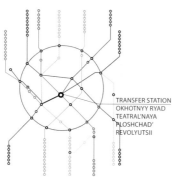

Moscow metro

15-minute walking distance

Public Sector Needs

The Moskva Collection is the retail portion of a larger project known as the Moskva Hotel, a renovated hotel dating from the Stalin era. It is strategically situated next to Red Square and the Kremlin, across the street from the Duma, the National Hotel, the historic Bolshoi Theatre and old Metropole Hotel, and a short walk from the G.U.M. and St. Basil's Cathedral. Located at the northern terminus of Tvserskaya Shosse—the primary entry road into the heart of Moscow from Sheremetevo Airport—it sits directly above a subway line, with a station entry on the face of the reconstructed building. Preservation of the property's image was a priority, as the City of Moscow mandated the maintenance of the historic appearance of the original building.

The renovation includes a new Four Seasons Hotel, with apartments for retired generals; a conference center; two levels of subterranean parking; and three levels of high-end couture retail shops.

Private Sector Needs

The retail development program, produced by OJSC "DecMos", called for three floors of refined, internationally branded shops, which would produce a sense of an elite destination. Providing flexibility to accommodate merchant needs while creating a sense of spaciousness to meet customer expectations was essential, as were convenient parking and customer comfort. Simplicity of form, clarity of movement, refinement of details, classic elegance and quality of materials were required to create differentiation.

Project Issues

Locating the new development above a transit tunnel necessitated the placement of an independent development structure that would span the tunnel, with control joints to assure that movement and vibrations from the trains could not be detected. Building code provisions, which required a separate means of vertical pedestrian conveyance, as well as separate exit stair shafts for each of the individual stacked uses, hampered the retail component. Further, no meaningful identification of the interior uses of the building would be allowed on the exterior façade. No natural light penetrated the public spaces of the building, which were located under a conference center and a large apartment block. No direct access from the subway station box into the project was allowed.

Exterior view

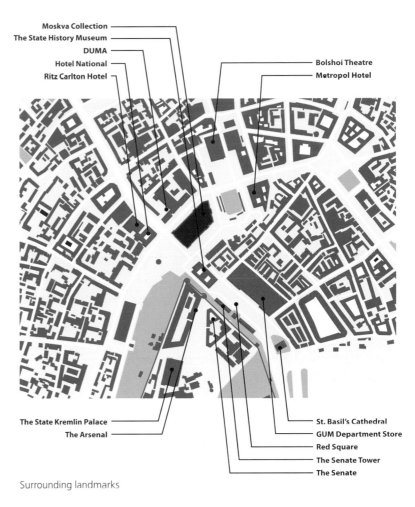

Moskva Collection
The State History Museum
DUMA
Hotel National
Ritz Carlton Hotel

Bolshoi Theatre
Metropol Hotel

The State Kremlin Palace
The Arsenal

St. Basil's Cathedral
GUM Department Store
Red Square
The Senate Tower
The Senate

Surrounding landmarks

Design Solutions

Although constrained above and below by structure, blast shafts, elevator shafts, exit stairs and mechanical rooms, the design carved out a single, coherent space, around which every shop is focused. In the absence of natural light, ceiling and bulkhead feature an elegant Lalique-like glass structure. The addition of a special entrance adjacent to the station exit provides linkage to the famous Moscow metro.

Public Benefits

The project brought a much-needed international five-star business hotel to the district next to the seat of government and close to the primary tourist destinations in Moscow. The high-end retail complex serves the customers of the Moskva Hotel and the neighboring Ritz-Carlton and Ararat Park Hyatt. Conveniently located directly above a transit station, this showpiece destination is easily accessible from the entire region.

Three-level retail galleria above the metro

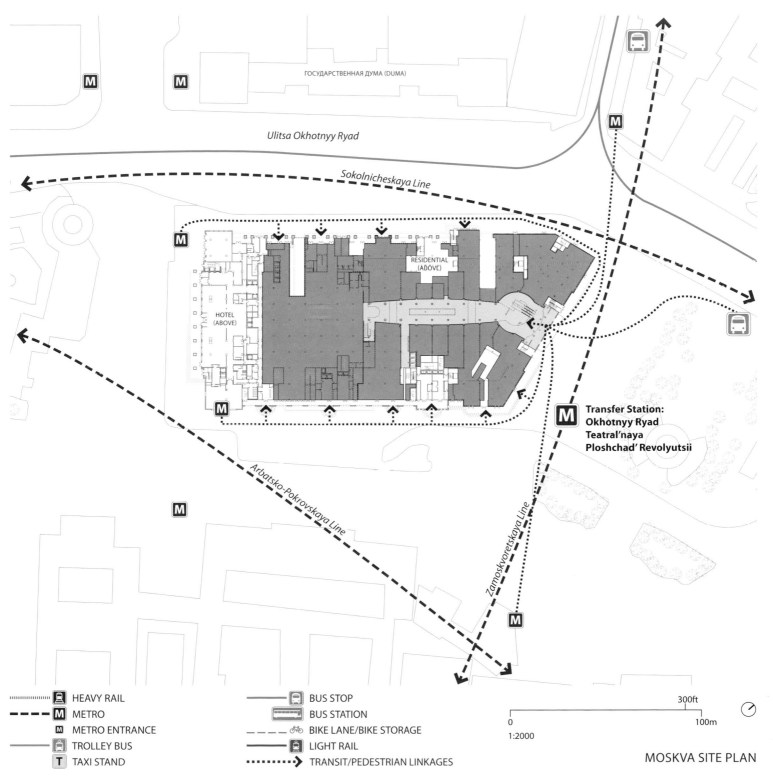

ГОСУДАРСТВЕННАЯ ДУМА (DUMA)

Ulitsa Okhotnyy Ryad

Sokolnicheskaya Line

RESIDENTIAL
(ABOVE)

HOTEL
(ABOVE)

Arbatsko-Pokrovskaya Line

Zamoskvoretskaya Line

**Transfer Station:
Okhotnyy Ryad
Teatral'naya
Ploshchad' Revolyutsii**

▥	HEAVY RAIL	
M	METRO	
M	METRO ENTRANCE	
	TROLLEY BUS	
T	TAXI STAND	

▤ BUS STOP	
▤ BUS STATION	
🚲 BIKE LANE/BIKE STORAGE	
🚲 LIGHT RAIL	
▸ TRANSIT/PEDESTRIAN LINKAGES	

300ft

0   100m

1:2000

MOSKVA SITE PLAN

Victoria City

Bucharest, Romania

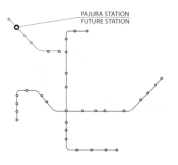

Bucharest metro

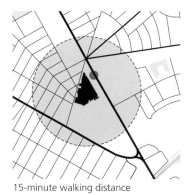

15-minute walking distance

Public Sector Needs

The Municipality of Bucharest sought to convert former industrial sites in the inner city to better use, while providing for sustainable growth and quality public spaces. The project, located on one of Bucharest's main boulevards connecting to the city center, is a prime example of meeting cultural, commercial and financial community needs.

Private Sector Needs

From a development standpoint, it was essential to create a flexible, well-functioning retail center with a positive image and identity, signature public spaces, direct access to the metro station on site, retail services, and with pedestrian access to neighboring blocks.

Project Issues

The project is located on a 13-acre (5.3-hectare) brownfield site approximately 4 miles (6.5 kilometers) from the city center. The triangular site lies adjacent to a metro station with two access points, as well as direct access to Bucuresti Noi Boulevard via Strada Triumfului on the northern side, and a new street on the southern side. Critical issues revolved around restrictions resulting from below-ground infrastructure and metro line facilities. There were also significant planning and massing requirements relating to the percentage of green space on site, height limitations, traffic solutions for the new streets and rights-of-way, and the virtual lack of back servicing access. In addition, the project has a dominant frontage and presence along the Bucuresti Noi Boulevard, with an 88-foot (27-meter) setback requirement to accommodate existing infrastructure. The western part of the site is bounded by a new road linking adjacent neighborhoods.

Design Solutions

The project creates a visual landmark that provides civic identity, appealing to both retailers and the community, with sculptural elements forming "cornerstones" at pedestrian gateways, and dining terraces along the boulevard. It also addresses several transit imperatives, including: incorporating and accommodating three modes of public transport; responding to the interactive relationships between retailers and customers, many of whom arrive via public transit; providing efficient parking distribution that minimizes cross-traffic conflict; and allowing for economic and efficient servicing.

Metro/retail linkage on Bucuresti Noi Blvd

Public Benefits

The community benefits from a project that provides connectivity between neighborhoods, as well as new public spaces, and new retail, dining, and leisure facilities. It improved the city's quality of life by turning a former brownfield site into a new landmark destination that fully utilizes Bucharest's metro, tram, bus and trolley bus system.

Aerial view

Interior mall

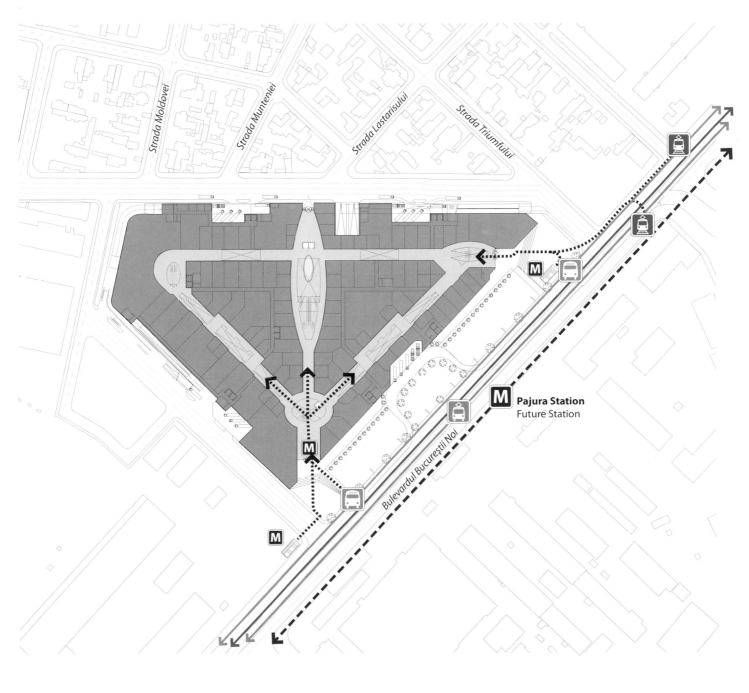

Strada Moldovei
Strada Munteniei
Strada Lastarisului
Strada Triumfului

Bulevardul Bucureștii Noi

M **Pajura Station**
Future Station

.... 🚊 HEAVY RAIL

– – – **M** METRO

▣ METRO ENTRANCE

🚃 TROLLEY BUS

T TAXI STAND

🚌 BUS STOP

🚌 BUS STATION

– – – 🚲 BIKE LANE/BIKE STORAGE

🚈 LIGHT RAIL

••••••► TRANSIT/PEDESTRIAN LINKAGES

300ft
0   100m
1:2500

VICTORIA CITY SITE PLAN

TRANSIT ORIENTED DEVELOPMENT 83

Mucha Centre

Prague, Czech Republic

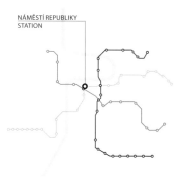

NÁMĚSTÍ REPUBLIKY
STATION

Prague metro

15-minute walking distance

Public Sector Needs

Prague is a well preserved historic Central European capital city which values its cultural heritage as a high priority. The city center, while vibrant, was not attracting local residents to shop in the downtown to satisfy the footfall potential of the district. Local subway, streetcar and bus transit systems converged at the site, but were underutilized and did not achieve ridership potential. The public sector desired a developer to produce an infill project at the intersection of two major downtown streets, and to restore the historic stables and barracks structure where Austrian Emperor Franz Josef quartered his troops and horses during their control of the city. Additionally, an adjacent chapel and town house were to be preserved and integrated into the scheme.

Private Sector Needs

The client, European Property Developers, desired to create a contemporary but sensitive urban infill-mixed-use, transit oriented development that took full advantage of a lower level connection to the subway and street level access for those arriving by streetcar and bus. The mix of uses would include an office building, five-star hotel, retail complex with dining facilities, and cinema.

Project Issues

The challenges of integrating a mixed-use program into the shell of four historic structures, and achieving street and below-grade linkages to the various public transit systems, needed to be balanced with the efficient and effective layout of each of the commercial uses. The significantly inclined site also needed to accommodate both private and service vehicles.

Design Solutions

Beginning with the transit connections, the project was planned to reinforce the urban fabric while introducing an unexpected and grand scale of interior spaces within. By achieving a "wow" experience inside, Mucha Centre, now called Palladium, delivers a sharply contrasting experience from what is available elsewhere in the city. A series of 26 allegorical mural paintings by Alfonse Mucha were to be incorporated into the project to attract tourist visitors utilizing public transportation.

Aerial view showing subway portal

Public Benefits

The city benefits from having a new economic engine driving the
revitalization of the community that surrounds the project site, all accessible
on three forms of public transit. Ridership on the transit lines is up—a
consequence of creating a station destination of unparalleled interest and
significance.

Plaza view showing tram and bus lines

Interior atrium

Office/Tram interface

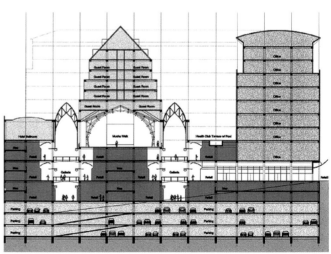

Section through office, hotel, retail and parking

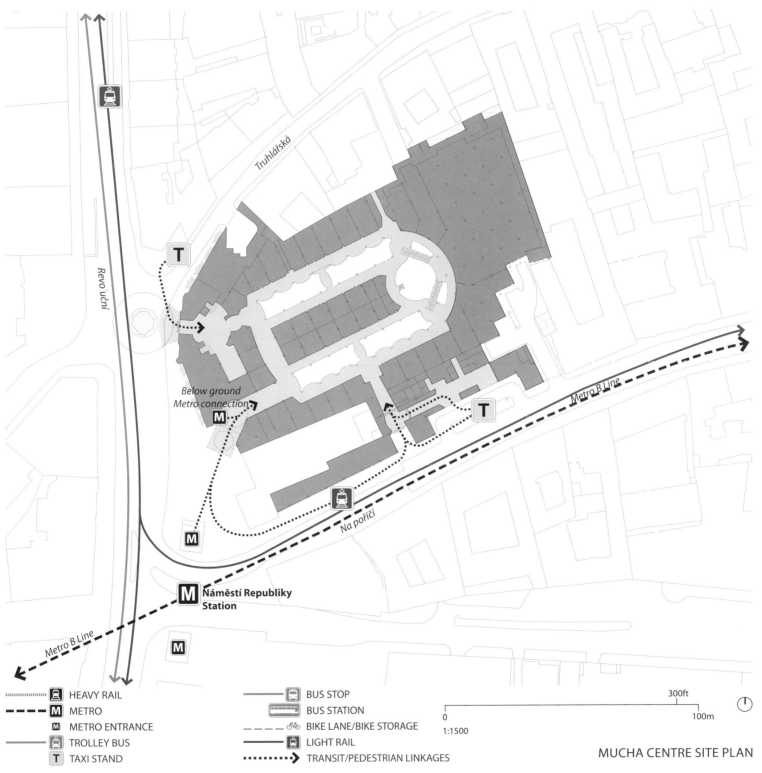

Truhlářská

Revo'uční

T

Below ground
Metro connection

M

M

Na poříčí

Metro B Line

Metro B Line

M **Náměstí Republiky Station**

M

	HEAVY RAIL		BUS STOP
M	METRO		BUS STATION
M	METRO ENTRANCE	🚲	BIKE LANE/BIKE STORAGE
	TROLLEY BUS		LIGHT RAIL
T	TAXI STAND	▸	TRANSIT/PEDESTRIAN LINKAGES

300ft

0   100m
1:1500

MUCHA CENTRE SITE PLAN

Gresham Station

Gresham, Oregon

CIVIC DRIVE
STATION

TriMet system

15-minute walking distance

Public Sector Needs

TriMet, the public transit agency in the Portland metropolitan region, produced one of the most highly utilized and customer-friendly public transit systems in the United States. Primarily comprised of light rail and buses, it was convenient and well accepted. Having adopted an Urban Growth Boundary to limit urban sprawl and encourage urban reinvestment, the City of Portland and TriMet were seeking infill projects that would create new destinations and generate increased ridership on the transit lines. To meet the needs of an avid bicycle-riding customer base, a bicycle park 'n' ride facility would be central to the concept.

Private Sector Needs

The developer, Winmar, envisioned a project with several retail product types—an enclosed, two-level fashion gallery; a single level, mid-market retail center; and a street-facing strip. The design, planned to meet tested retail industry standards, had to be cost effective to build. The functionally efficient development—with well-distributed anchor stores, shops, services, and restaurants—needed to accommodate the regional fashion center, and an entertainment center and civic space for the annual jazz festival, as well as the large number of projected transit customers.

Project Issues

The project is located on a terraced site, comprised of two flat plateaus separated by a steep incline, and bifurcated by a light rail line that runs along a north–south directional vector at the base of the incline, terminating at the township of Gresham. The new Gresham Station development, intended to attract riders from both Gresham and Portland, is located at a mid-point in the project. Resolving the intrusion of the light rail through the heart of the site, and the 20-foot (6-meter) vertical grade separation from east to west, posed a significant challenge.

Design Solutions

The concept was to convert the site challenges into design opportunities. The light rail train arrives at the project at grade level, and upon entry, the building's glass safety doors automatically shut. When the station is not in use, the doors open, allowing customers to cross over the tracks as pedestrians. Utilizing the station as a project hub, defined by a glass "round house" that evokes historic railroad station imagery, all programmatic elements— fashion galleria, mid-market retail, cinema, food hall, civic space, performance space—feed

Center court "round house" showing light rail station connection

from and connect to that pivotal point. Located on the ground level, the light rail provides customers with direct access to the first floor of the retail galleria to the east, and the outdoor civic and performing space to the north. One level up the escalators, customers arrive at the second level of fashion retail and the mid-market center to the west. The cinema and food hall are located up one additional escalator run, directly above the tracks, with a spectacular view of Mt. Jefferson. Destination has reinforced public transit desirability.

Public Benefits

TriMet commented that with the design concept and supporting imagery, they could petition positively to the U.S. Government Urban Mass Transit Authority for development funds. The concept of creating a collection of civic destinations—all fed from a light rail transit station—was compelling, and the 18-hour retail/dining/entertainment/civic program of the project was designed to create a multi-valent draw.

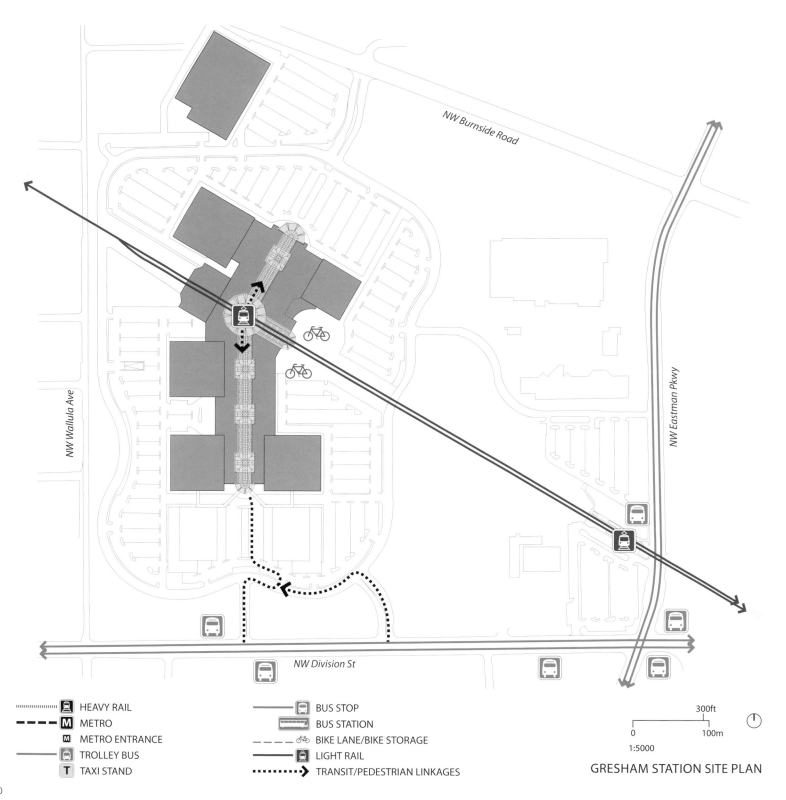

NW Burnside Road

NW Wallula Ave

NW Eastman Pkwy

NW Division St

	HEAVY RAIL		BUS STOP
M	METRO		BUS STATION
M	METRO ENTRANCE		BIKE LANE/BIKE STORAGE
	TROLLEY BUS		LIGHT RAIL
T	TAXI STAND		TRANSIT/PEDESTRIAN LINKAGES

300ft

0   100m

1:5000

GRESHAM STATION SITE PLAN

Outdoor civic plaza

Center court section showing light rail integration

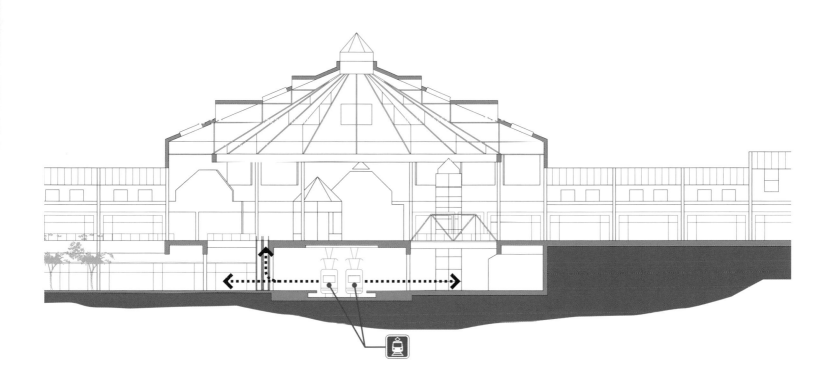

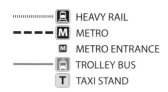

Walsin Mixed-use Complex

Jinan, China

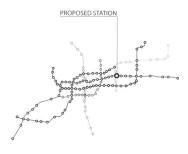

PROPOSED STATION

Jinan metro

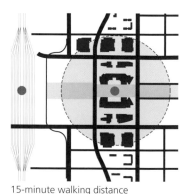

15-minute walking distance

Public Sector Needs

As China prepared to implement a national transportation infrastructure plan, Jinan, a second-tier city of six million inhabitants figured prominently in the plan. The capital of Shandong Province, strategically located midway between Beijing and Shanghai, it is a center of residential, educational and industrial growth.

On the western edge of the city, a large site, once occupied by a military air base, plays host to the new urban development. The city planners have developed a master plan to provide a 50 percent expansion of the existing downtown and supporting urban areas. The new urban core is anchored on its far west edge by the new Jinan high-speed rail station, the only stop between the two mega-cities. The station, now fully operational, hosts not only the high-speed train, but also other national and regional trains, several subway lines, a bus station and significant taxi stand.

As the multi-square kilometer site will ultimately host many thousands of residential units, commercial office space, retail, restaurants, cultural facilities and public parks among other uses, the public sector sought a major development to serve as a catalyst for the new development area and to create a sense of destination for the new high-tech station. Envisioning a major public green extending from the rail station, the public sector desired that this grand gesture be respected by all developments located along the new civic axis.

Private Sector Needs

The developer, Walsin, envisioned a high-density, mixed-use project that would be situated virtually at the doorstep of the new multi-modal hub. As the site straddles the new east–west subway line linking the high-speed rail station to the heart of the historic downtown, and as the project would be bifurcated by the requirement for continuous open green space, access from four subway concourse portals was deemed both desirable and essential in order to energize the four portals to the mixed-use project. Additionally, a visual and physical connection with the transit hub was an urban design objective.

Project Issues

When projects are infrastructure-led, the creation of human-scaled development and spaces are often the greatest challenges. While great cities have evolved over time, enriched by the layers of history and moments of visual dissonance, spontaneous cities struggle to achieve both the visual richness and authenticity that time brings.

Aerial view showing high-speed rail and heavy rail station

Design Solutions

Historic Chinese courtyard buildings, both at an epic and more modest scale, have long provided a "civicness" that creates a sense of destination. Arriving at a magnificent transit station may evoke the city's portal, but the gesture of welcome comes from the first impression upon departing the front door. The complex is designed in many layers of visual interest, familiarity, and discovery. Based on centuries-old planning concepts of space and movement, it contains many of the traditional Chinese planning and building design elements—reinterpreted in a 21st-century idiom.

Public Benefits

A rich and diverse range of both public uses and spaces makes the design of the Walsin Jinan Mixed-use Complex easily accessible to both transit users and neighboring communities alike. Linking directly to adjacent streets, to the subway, and to the railroad station, urban integration is achieved at the highest level of planning and design.

View from high-speed rail and heavy rail station

Aerial view

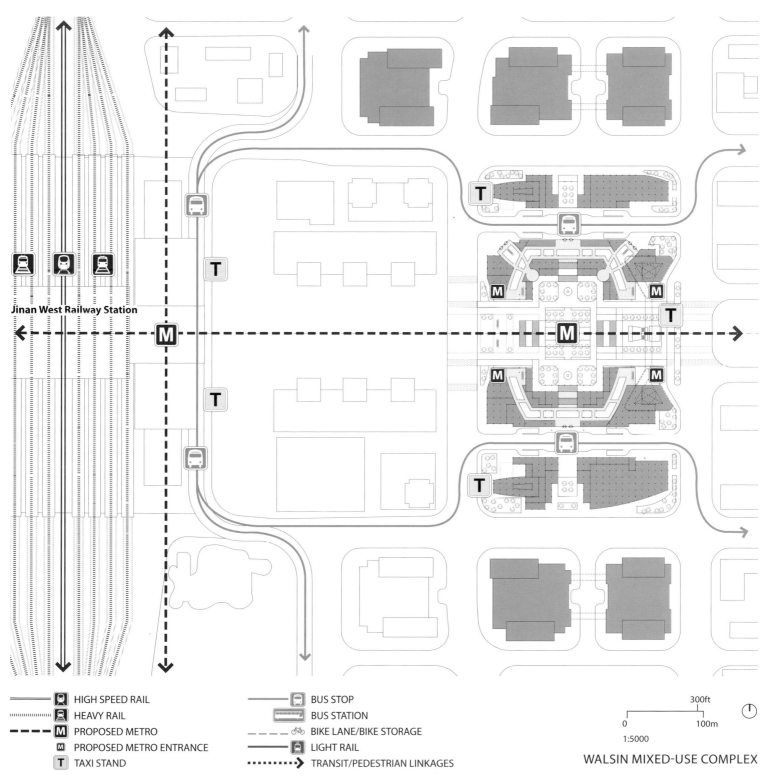

Jinan West Railway Station

HIGH SPEED RAIL
HEAVY RAIL
PROPOSED METRO
PROPOSED METRO ENTRANCE
TAXI STAND

BUS STOP
BUS STATION
BIKE LANE/BIKE STORAGE
LIGHT RAIL
TRANSIT/PEDESTRIAN LINKAGES

300ft

0   100m

1:5000

WALSIN MIXED-USE COMPLEX

TRANSIT ADJACENT DEVELOPMENT

Transit Adjacent Development

Many projects that thrive due to their proximity to transit stations do not have direct links to them. A Transit Adjacent Development (TAD) may be situated across the street from a station entrance, or even a block away; nonetheless, it must have immediate and convenient access to and reliance on the transit station.

The examples here were designed with an understanding of transit agency needs, which ensured that connections to the station boxes did not interfere with the safe operation of those stations. Considerations centered on the desire of the transit authority and the developers for linkage between the transit stations and the developments. In all cases, existing transit lines—including high-speed train, passenger rail, subway, light rail, bus and taxi stands—were operational or in construction concurrently. Like the TOD examples, the construction that occurred adjacent to the transit stations responded to the functional, environmental, and emergency needs of the transit stations, as well as the need to accommodate vibration and noise. Again, the convenient conversion of passenger traffic leaving the transit realm into customer traffic entering the commercial development was of mutual benefit.

While some may argue that TADs achieve fewer community objectives than TODs, nevertheless, when they are programmatically altered in a significant way as a consequence of their adjacencies, they offer comparable benefits to direct transit developments. Taking the longer view, development beyond the single focal point station site offers the additional benefit of a ripple effect, with the potential of transforming whole neighborhoods. This, in turn, provides increased ridership.

Examples include constructed and designed projects in Asia; Eastern, Central and Western Europe; and the United States.

CentralWorld
Bangkok, Thailand

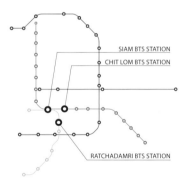

SIAM BTS STATION
CHIT LOM BTS STATION
RATCHADAMRI BTS STATION

Bangkok metro

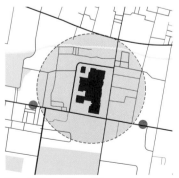

15-minute walking distance

Public Sector Needs
Traffic in Bangkok is congested to the point that it is impossible to schedule meetings and expect people to arrive on time reliably. As a consequence, the government encourages the use of public transit and sponsors more intense urban regeneration. The public sector wanted each station of its overhead train to be developed into a major destination hub for office, retail, hospitality, dining and public gathering space.

Private Sector Needs
Central Pattana (CPN), the client/owner of CentralWorld (the former World Trade Center) was faced with the challenge of bringing customers into the site, which could only be accessed on two sides, both off one of the most congested intersections in the city. There was a serious need to create a better bus service, easier vehicular access, and, more importantly, a more direct connection to the above-grade rail.

Project Issues
The project site was wide and deep, and the new proposed uses—hotel, convention center, office tower—would need street frontage to be commercially viable. Additionally, the overhead commuter rail was disconnected from the project, requiring patrons to descend or ascend approximately 20 feet (6 meters) to the walking platform in order to access the development.

Solutions
The site was large enough to allow for a new multi-lane roadway to provide access for buses, taxis, personal vehicles, and service and emergency vehicles to the two under-served sides of the property, which would bring front door access to a new hotel, convention center, and office building. The addition of a covered bridge, linking a new three-level retail galleria and three-story office building lobby to the covered pedestrian walkway, allows passengers stopping at either of the two stations to gain direct access into the mixed-use complex with protection from intense summer sun or the seasonal rains.

Overall exterior

Public Benefits

For riders of both rail and bus public transit there was now protected direct access to every function of this 8.5-million-square-foot (2,590,800-square-meter) mixed-use project. The least utilized pedestrian entrance, upon being connected to the above-grade rail and pedestrian walkway, became the number one project portal according to office building and retail center footfall counts. Affirmative linkage to public transit created opportunity and fulfilled demand.

Plaza, office lobby exterior

Linkage from metro into retail and office tower lobby

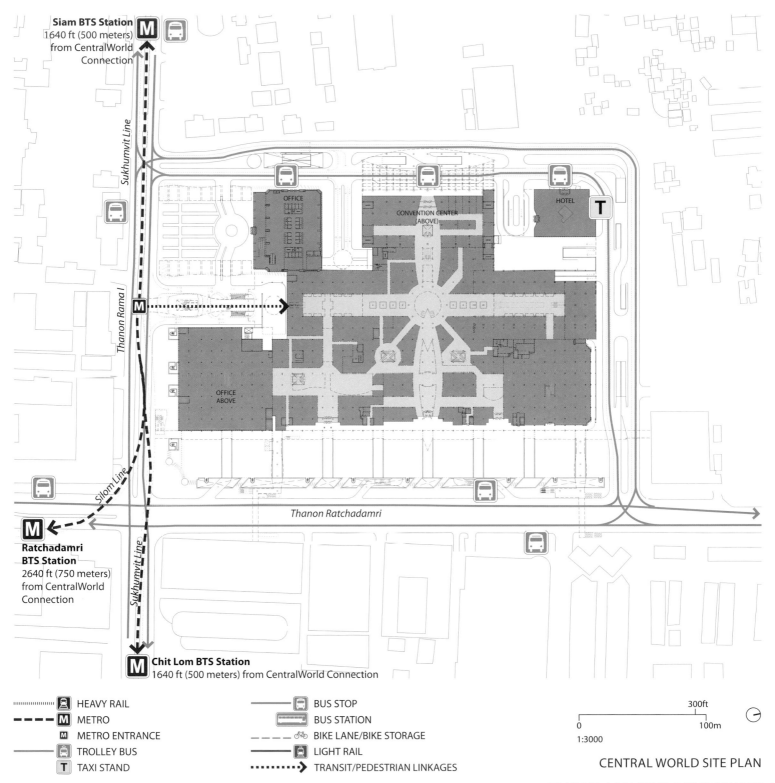

Siam BTS Station
1640 ft (500 meters)
from CentralWorld
Connection

Sukhumvit Line

Thanon Rama I

Silom Line

Sukhumvit Line

OFFICE

CONVENTION CENTER
(ABOVE)

HOTEL

T

OFFICE
ABOVE

**Ratchadamri
BTS Station**
2640 ft (750 meters)
from CentralWorld
Connection

Thanon Ratchadamri

Chit Lom BTS Station
1640 ft (500 meters) from CentralWorld Connection

HEAVY RAIL

METRO

METRO ENTRANCE

TROLLEY BUS

T   TAXI STAND

BUS STOP

BUS STATION

BIKE LANE/BIKE STORAGE

LIGHT RAIL

TRANSIT/PEDESTRIAN LINKAGES

300ft

0   100m
1:3000

CENTRAL WORLD SITE PLAN

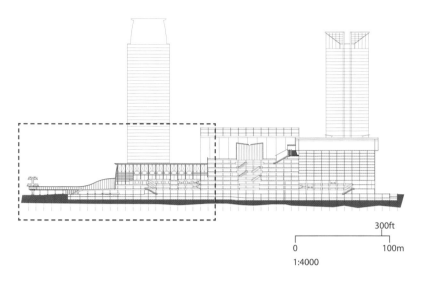

300ft
0 —— 100m
1:4000

Interior of new high-end retail storefronts

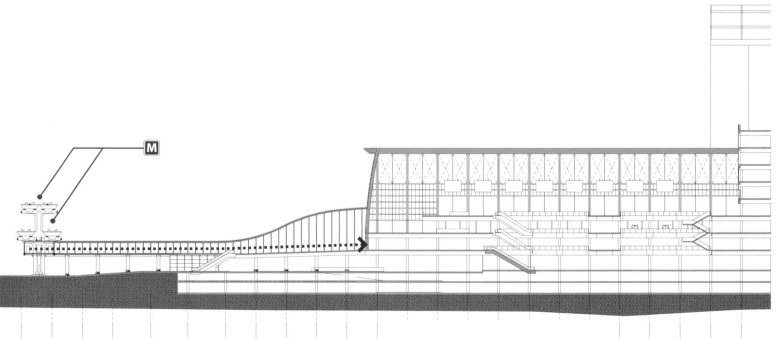

	HEAVY RAIL		BUS STOP
M	METRO		BUS STATION
M	METRO ENTRANCE		BIKE LANE/BIKE STORAGE
	TROLLEY BUS		LIGHT RAIL
T	TAXI STAND	·······>	TRANSIT/PEDESTRIAN LINKAGES

150ft
0 —— 50m
1:1000

CENTRAL WORLD SECTION

Transit bridge connection to project entry

Mall interior atrium

Interior circulation facing plaza

Nieuw Hoog Catharijne
Utrecht, The Netherlands

The Netherlands rail

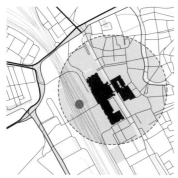

15-minute walking distance

Public Sector Needs

Hoog Catharijne was an existing 3.77-million-square-foot (350,00-square-meter) mixed-use project in the heart of Utrecht. With 30 million retail visitors each year, it was the most visited shopping center in The Netherlands. The expanded project is a major component of the City of Utrecht's new master plan for one of the largest urban retail/leisure redevelopments in northern Europe, which will create a vibrant and durable new center that connects the city center with the railway station. Redevelopment objectives included: improving quality and safety, strengthening Utrecht's urban and economic role, enhancing accessibility to the city by a wide range of transport methods, and exploiting the fact that Utrecht is the largest public transport interchange in The Netherlands.

Private Sector Needs

From a development standpoint, it was essential to expand the retail and leisure offer, making it home to new civic spaces, and connecting the central train station with the historic medieval city center. The New Hoog Catharijne (NHC) plan, approved by the City, was to increase Hoog Catharijne's existing 1.4-million-square-foot (130,000-square-meter) retail/leisure offer by 538,000 square feet (50,000 square meters), to accommodate the 100,000 growth in population, and the anticipated increase of passengers going through Utrecht's central train station to 100 million by 2030.

Project Issues

Critical issues included the three-dimensional coordination of existing and proposed transit and related infrastructures, articulating the development around historical monuments, countering the negative perception of the project as a "concrete bunker" with inactive and inhospitable street frontages, and addressing station arrival areas located above the city's existing streets and squares.

Design Solutions

The urban and architectural design enhances connectivity between the medieval city, Utrecht's central station, and the new developments to the west of the city center. The project is conceived as a collection of clearly defined civic spaces connected by two urban retail passages with direct linkage to multiple modes of public transit. The scale of the spaces and landmarks that define the development respond to the physical, cultural and historic context of the city, as well as its vision for the future, which includes transit accessibility.

Linkage of transit station to retail, hotel, museum, "city room" and residential

These include direct rail and bus connections to Schiphol International Airport; local, regional, national and international trains; light rail that connects surrounding communities; Pan-European, regional, local and shuttle buses; taxis; kiss 'n' ride; 5,000 on-site parking spaces; and 22,000 bike parking stalls.

Public Benefits
NHC has become the gateway to and from Utrecht via the largest multi-modal public transit hub in the nation. It plays a pivotal role in achieving the objectives of the City's master plan, which also includes: residential and office components; the refurbishment of the historic Vredenburg Square; the reintroduction of the medieval city canal, which was covered by roadways in the 1970s; the refurbishment and expansion of the music palace and central station; and the expansion of the adjacent convention center. This transit-oriented development is being realized through a series of public–private partnerships. Total investment is estimated to be €3.2 billion, of which approximately two-thirds is privately funded.

Linkage of transit station to retail, hotel, museum, "city room" and residential

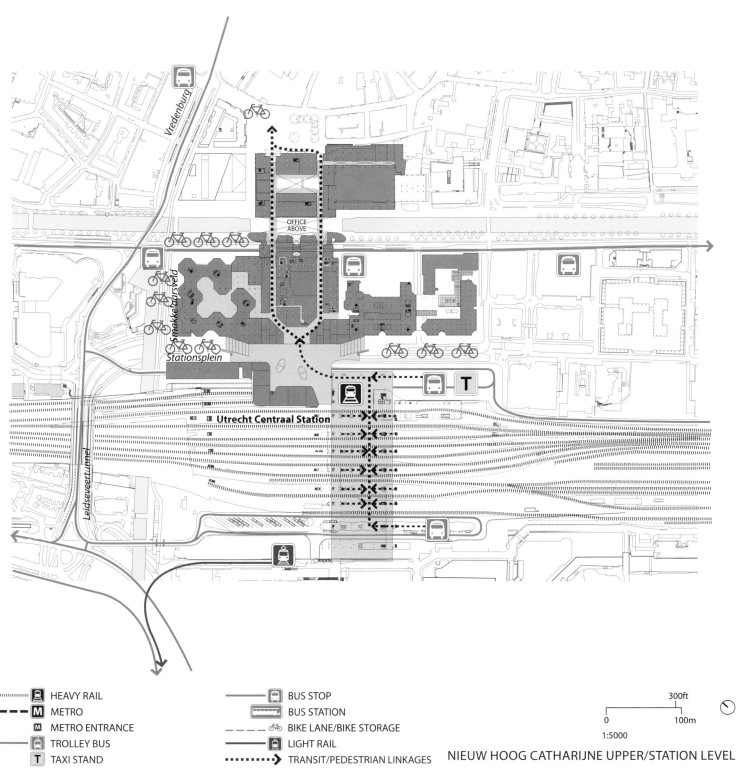

Vredenburg

OFFICE
ABOVE

Smakkelaarsveld

Stationsplein

Leidseveertunnel

Utrecht Centraal Station

	HEAVY RAIL		BUS STOP
M	METRO		BUS STATION
M	METRO ENTRANCE		BIKE LANE/BIKE STORAGE
	TROLLEY BUS		LIGHT RAIL
T	TAXI STAND		TRANSIT/PEDESTRIAN LINKAGES

300ft

0   100m

1:5000

"City Room" civic space

Medieval plaza residential

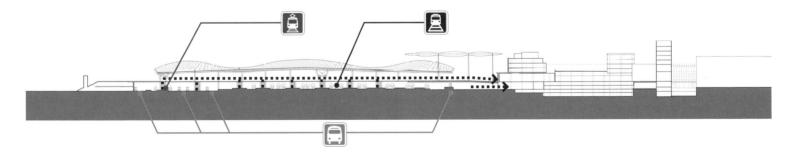

 HEAVY RAIL
M METRO
M METRO ENTRANCE
TROLLEY BUS
T TAXI STAND

 BUS STOP
BUS STATION
BIKE LANE/BIKE STORAGE
LIGHT RAIL
TRANSIT/PEDESTRIAN LINKAGES

300ft
0   100m
1:3000

NIEUW HOOG CATHARIJNE SECTION

TRANSIT ADJACENT DEVELOPMENT 113

The Shops at Tanforan
San Bruno, California

Bay Area Rapid Transit (BART)

15-minute walking distance

Public Sector Needs
When the Bay Area Rapid Transit (BART) extended its service south to the international airport, the City of San Bruno, which was the last stop before the San Francisco International Airport, saw an opportunity to spur development and bring more people to the city. The San Bruno stop was adjacent to the Tanforan Mall, which was being redeveloped. If riders could be turned into shoppers the city would become an attractive destination just minutes from the airport and would benefit from increased sales tax revenue.

Private Sector Needs
The developer, Wattson Breevast, had recently acquired the dated shopping center and recognized that the presence of the new BART station immediately to the east of the property, a bus transfer station at what had been the back of the property, and the expanded influence of the airport had the potential to boost sales. They needed a "front door" facing the station that would welcome passengers with ease of access and a mix of transit related retail, restaurant and entertainment destinations as well as the expanded retail offerings of the revitalized center.

Project Issues
The center now needed two distinct entrances—one facing the BART station and the other facing the highway. The existing center was in poor condition, suffering from neglect as well as poor planning. Originally designed to a classic dumbbell plan, with a department store anchoring either end, the addition of a third anchor connected by shops in a side mall perpendicular to, but narrower than, the original created awkward lease depths and poor navigation.

Design Solutions
The 1.6-million-square-foot (487,680-square-meter) expansion transformed the center into a multi-modal, mixed-use commercial complex that showcases grand civic spaces and transit-related retail opportunities that are closely linked to the BART station and the surrounding neighborhood. An outdoor plaza with restaurants, a bookstore, and a water feature provides access to the complex from the street. Inside the redesigned concourses, two levels of shops are organized around a spacious, light-filled central courtyard that connects to the BART station entry.

East entrance

Interior of west entrance facing BART station

Just north of this new entry at the BART station, a new parking structure was added, with a multi-screen cinema sited directly above it. Cinema customers purchase their tickets on the second level of the mall entry structure, bringing the many cinemagoers into the mall on their way in and out of the movies. On the west façade of the building, facing the city street, a new restaurant and two-level bookstore flank the new, bold entrance structure. Further, the lower level bookstore utilizes the deep basement space that was previously vacant.

Public Benefits
San Bruno gained a destination that attracts shoppers from the entire south San Francisco region and travelers from the airport with long layovers, many of them arriving by BART, whose passenger numbers have enjoyed a boost due to the convenience of this entertainment/dining destination.

Exterior showing mall expansion and transit integration

Exterior showing mall expansion and transit integration

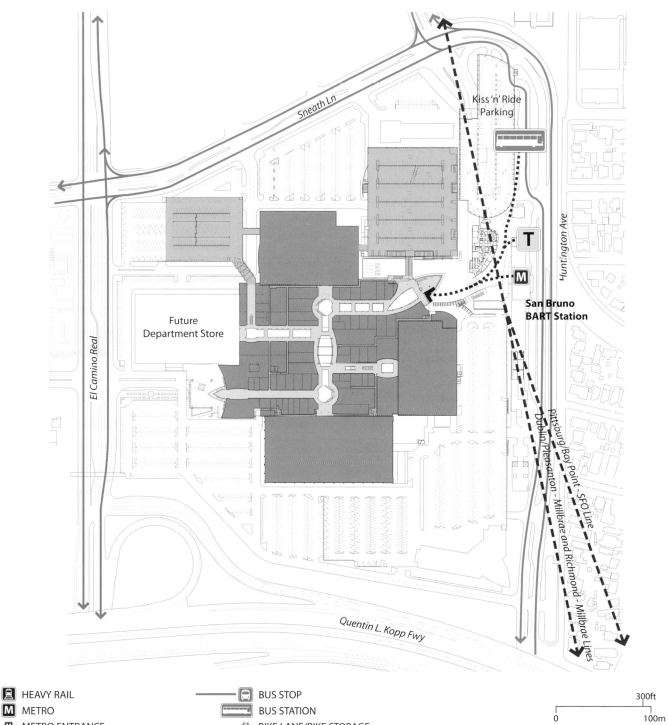

Sneath Ln

Kiss 'n' Ride Parking

El Camino Real

Future Department Store

Huntington Ave

T

M

San Bruno BART Station

Pittsburg/Bay Point - SFO Line
Dublin/Pleasanton - Millbrae and Richmond - Millbrae Lines

Quentin L. Kopp Fwy

▨	HEAVY RAIL	▨ BUS STOP
M	METRO	▨ BUS STATION
M	METRO ENTRANCE	🚲 BIKE LANE/BIKE STORAGE
▨	TROLLEY BUS	▨ LIGHT RAIL
T	TAXI STAND	TRANSIT/PEDESTRIAN LINKAGES

300ft

0   100m

1:4000

THE SHOPS AT TANFORAN SITE PLAN

The Atrium at Kursky Station

Moscow, Russia

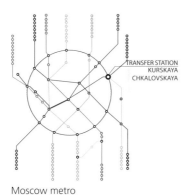

Moscow metro

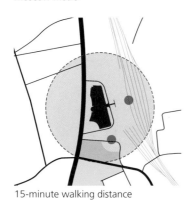

15-minute walking distance

Public Sector Needs

One of the earliest contemporary Western retail projects developed as Russia moved to a market economy, The Atrium sought to address a series of public sector issues. First, the City Architect had imposed planning and building massing requirements on the site. Second, the multiple transit elements—long haul railroad, regional railroad, three subway lines, a streetcar line, bus lines, and a taxi stand—which brought some 675,000 people per day past the site, all needed to be integrated into the design scheme. Third, the mayor requested that the building, located on the historic Garden Ring, be not of a contemporary design, but evoke the character of the 19th-century context.

Private Sector Needs

First-time developers, Engeocom, sought to maximize the income-producing area on the site, within the planning and zoning guidelines. They also wanted a project that, while groundbreaking for the Russian retail industry, would endure the rapid evolution of building type as the country evolved from a command to a market economy.

Project Issues

With practically no history in the development of market-driven buildings, the City of Moscow building department was very conservative in its approach to the design. Additionally, since the building was to be constructed above a subway line, the structure had to span the subway tunnel as it angled through the site.

Design Solutions

The building was designed to function as a state-of-the-art retail/entertainment/dining project, fronting proudly on the Garden Ring, connecting at grade and above grade to the railroad and subway lines. The bus station and taxi stand access directly into the lower retail mall level, and the streetcar and street bus deliver customers directly to the second retail level.

Public Benefits

As the first retail center in democratic Russia designed by Western architects, The Atrium was the first to offer customers a view of western products and shopping protocol. Integrally connected to five separate forms of public transit, the building also set the bar for all future transit-oriented retail development in Russia.

Interior atrium

Glass bridge transit connection

Interior atrium view

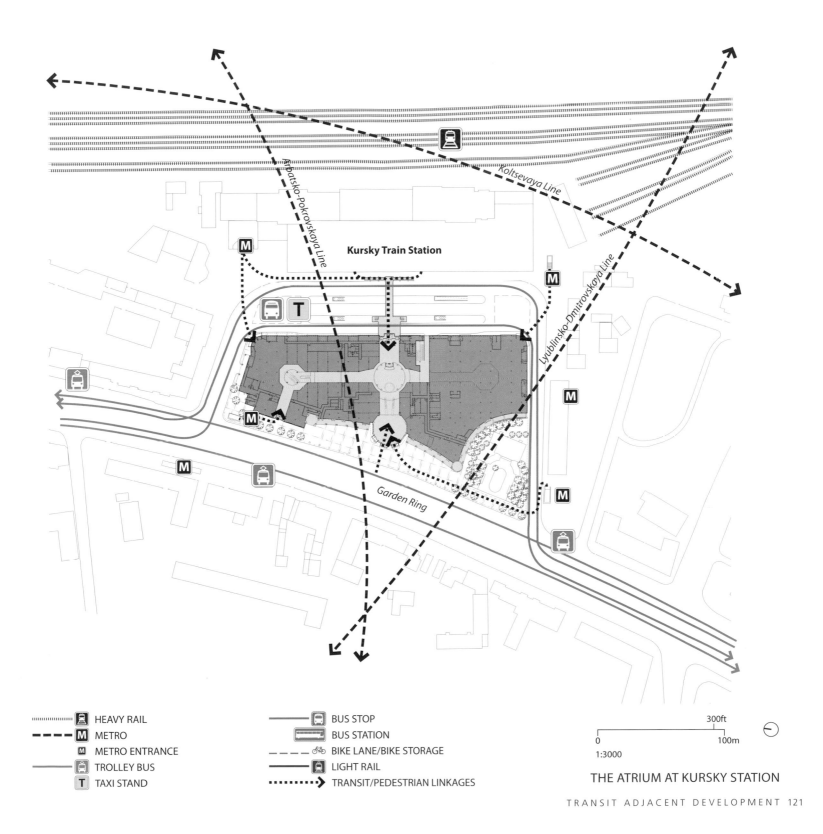

Kursky Train Station

Arbatsko-Pokrovskaya Line

Koltsevaya Line

Lyublinsko-Dmitrovskaya Line

Garden Ring

	HEAVY RAIL		BUS STOP
M	METRO		BUS STATION
M	METRO ENTRANCE		BIKE LANE/BIKE STORAGE
	TROLLEY BUS		LIGHT RAIL
T	TAXI STAND		TRANSIT/PEDESTRIAN LINKAGES

300ft

0   100m

1:3000

THE ATRIUM AT KURSKY STATION

Yasenevo

Moscow, Russia

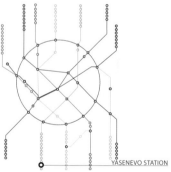

Moscow metro

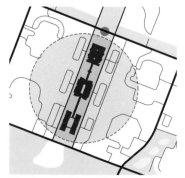

15-minute walking distance

Public Sector Needs

The City of Moscow planning officials mandated that the proposed mixed-use, transit-adjacent development respond to its context in several ways. First, it should make a convenient connection to the metro subway system below and above grade. Second, the on-site bus transfer parking lot should remain but be substantially improved. Third, the open space between existing Soviet-era housing blocks should be continued through the commercial site. Fourth, a leisure function should be added to the development program, to serve the neighboring communities.

Private Sector Needs

The developer, a partnership between OST Group and Simon-Ivanhoe, sought a mixed-use, infill project that would draw customers from a greater distance via the existing subway and enhanced bus transfer systems. Office buildings, retail, dining and leisure would occupy three blocks of the elongated site, permeated by the open park to create a community connection.

Project Issues

Beyond the significant slope of the site, the challenges of distributing retail and office uses adjacent to one another, and servicing them properly while exposing no "back sides" to the adjoining residential property, were significant. Connecting to the transit uses in a manner that allowed the project to present its best face to the primary avenue also posed logistical issues in the design process.

Design Solutions

Using the inclination of the site, the design creates two entry points off the major avenue. The lower level allows both subway and bus customers to reach the project under protection of the civic plaza, which sits above. From that plaza, customers can access the second level of shops. Visitors to the offices can access those buildings from the retail galleria or directly from the street. Service corridors for both uses are located between them, and are fed from service docks under the footprint of the office buildings.

View south from Block 1

Public Benefits

The community gained a transit-oriented mixed-use amenity that serves business, shopping, dining, entertainment and leisure needs, while preserving the historic character of the housing development in which it sits. With the addition of this new destination servicing the adjacent and nearby communities, ridership on the transit lines is expected to increase.

Project entrance on Block 3

Aerial view of Block 3

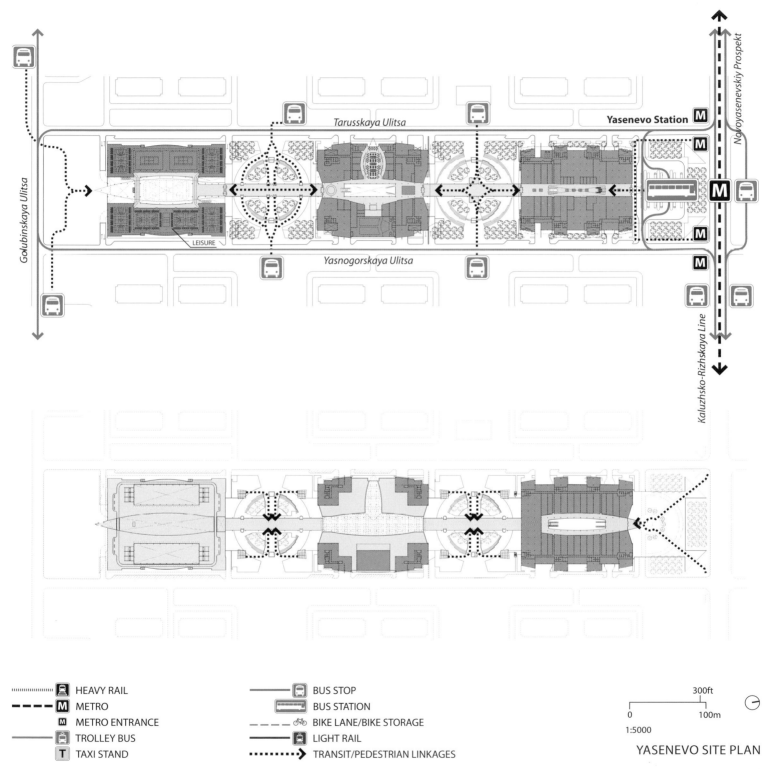

Golubinskaya Ulitsa

Tarusskaya Ulitsa

Yasenevo Station Ⓜ

Novoyasenevskiy Prospekt

LEISURE

Yasnogorskaya Ulitsa

Kaluzhsko-Rizhskaya Line

▥ HEAVY RAIL		🚌 BUS STOP	
Ⓜ METRO		🚍 BUS STATION	
Ⓜ METRO ENTRANCE		🚲 BIKE LANE/BIKE STORAGE	
🚎 TROLLEY BUS		🚈 LIGHT RAIL	
Ⓣ TAXI STAND		▶ TRANSIT/PEDESTRIAN LINKAGES	

300ft

0   100m

1:5000

YASENEVO SITE PLAN

Wuhan Shimao Carnival

Wuhan, China

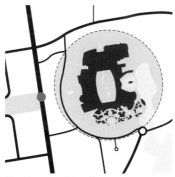

15-minute walking distance

Public Sector Needs

Located in the Wen Ling Peninsula in suburban Wuhan Hubei Province, surrounded by the region's network of lakes and rivers, Wuhan Shimao Carnival is slated to be a key player in a newly developing district with an emphasis on preserving, protecting and enhancing the natural environment. With a vision of creating a premier tourist destination for the region, the program for the property includes a vibrant mix of entertainment and leisure activities, including an amusement park, as well as a full range of retail. To ensure regional access to the destination, the site is host to a metro station along a planned transit line.

Private Sector Needs

Located at the eastern terminus, the district's major open space axis, Wuhan Carnival needed linkage to the civic functions that would define that space in the future, as well as a major point of pedestrian access. From the development perspective, the availability of transit to the site and ease of access from the train and bus stations to the activities at Wuhan Carnival were critical to the success of the project and satisfy the linkage requirement.

Project Issues

Given the scale of the development and the variety of attractions, it was important that the metro and bus station be integrated into the overall plan and not be perceived as auxiliary to the program. However, the metro station site was located at the far western end of the east–west axis that defines the project, creating an opportunity for a positive civic gesture, in the form of a major forecourt and grand entry, to ensure pedestrian interaction between the two.

Design Solutions

Considering the station as the point of access and departure for the development, the design embraces the station by creating a gracious forecourt that fronts a sequence of processional spaces leading to the heart of the amusement center. From there the freshly arrived passengers can observe all of the leisure and entertainment activities, as well as the sight of the adjacent lake with its Ferris wheel and observation point with views of the region's natural surroundings. The amusement park is surrounded by offerings that include a hypermarket, home furnishings center, sporting goods store, specialty retail, an Imax cinema, and a family-oriented three-star hotel. The venue design takes advantage of its natural setting with a mix of indoor and outdoor environments.

Aerial view

Public Benefits

The lively mix of attractions at the 500,000 square meter destination makes
a compelling draw for visitors from around the region, many of whom will
opt for the ease of to-the-door public transit options.

Interior view of upper level

Exterior view of entertainment courtyard

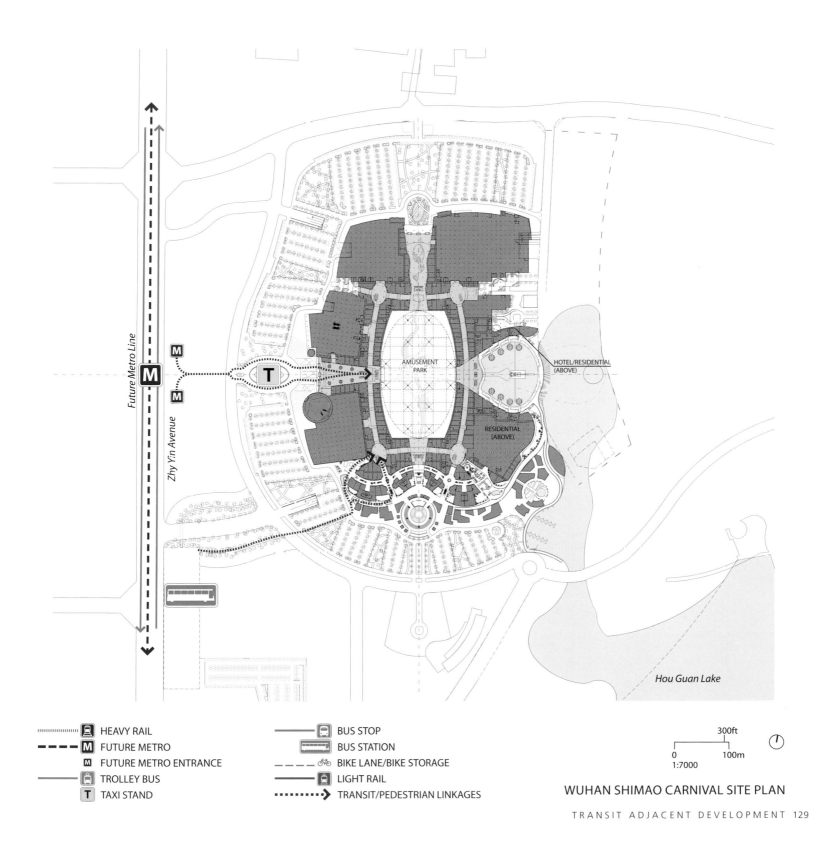

Future Metro Line

Zhy Yin Avenue

AMUSEMENT PARK

HOTEL/RESIDENTIAL
(ABOVE)

RESIDENTIAL
(ABOVE)

Hou Guan Lake

⚊⚊⚊ 🚆	HEAVY RAIL	⚊⚊ 🚌	BUS STOP
⚊ ⚊ Ⓜ	FUTURE METRO	⚊⚊ 🚍	BUS STATION
Ⓜ	FUTURE METRO ENTRANCE	⚊ ⚊ 🚲	BIKE LANE/BIKE STORAGE
🚎	TROLLEY BUS	⚊⚊ 🚈	LIGHT RAIL
Ⓣ	TAXI STAND	▪▪▪▪▪▶	TRANSIT/PEDESTRIAN LINKAGES

300ft

0   100m
1:7000

WUHAN SHIMAO CARNIVAL SITE PLAN

Buchanan Galleries
Glasgow, Scotland

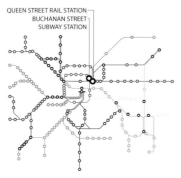

QUEEN STREET RAIL STATION
BUCHANAN STREET
SUBWAY STATION

Scotland rail and subway

15-minute walking distance

Public Sector Needs

The City of Glasgow has a mature and comprehensive mass transit network encompassing air, rail, road, and subway. Prior to 1962, the city was also served by trams. Much of the land utilized by transit stations and rights-of-way is in prime locations within the city, with potential for better use. Such is the case with Buchanan Galleries, located in the heart of Glasgow's city center, next to the Buchanan bus station, Buchanan Street subway station, and Queen Street rail station, with direct access to the prime retail axes of Buchanan Street and Sauchiehall Street. The transit agency sought to create greater integration between their hub and the balance of the city.

Private Sector Needs

With strong tenant demand and a supportive council, Buchanan Galleries had the potential to expand its floor area to an extent that would mutually benefit the Buchanan Partnership and the urban heart of Glasgow. The areas for this expansion rested largely on the properties of the Buchanan bus station and Queen Street rail station, both controlled by the local transit authority, the Strathclyde Partnership for Transport. With the right design, the Buchanan Galleries had the potential to add up to 750,000 square feet (228,600 square meters), thereby retaining market dominance.

Project Issues

Critical issues revolved around the limitations of working above and adjacent to existing transit infrastructure, while maintaining the operations of the existing bus, subway, and rail transit systems. In addition, project access from the transit nodes had to be optimized both in function and civic quality. Issues relating to car parking, servicing and safety were paramount. The City also had urban design concerns regarding the architectural and historic building context.

Design Solutions

The master plan was defined by the greater context of Glasgow's civic spaces and urban fabric, which informed the expansion of Buchanan Galleries' existing retail offer while improving the project's relationship to the existing modes of transit. Plans to connect the segregated transit—heavy rail, subway, tram and bus—by modifications and additions to the existing retail building, promises a better connected, healthier and more vital urban core.

Project gateway and subway entrance

Public Benefits

The project, at the heart of urban Glasgow, is locally, regionally, and nationally connected via transit. With the redevelopment of Buchanan Galleries, new civic spaces worthy of Glasgow's rich heritage would be reclaimed from previously utilitarian and industrial sites. The expanded Buchanan Galleries would provide an enriched cultural, commercial and lifestyle offer in the heart of the city for the tens of millions of passengers that use Glasgow's transit system each year.

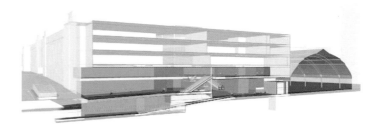

Section showing transit connections

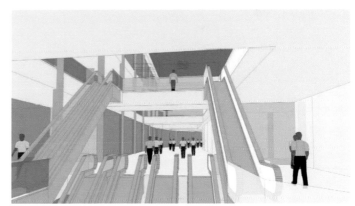

Interior circulation

Interior circulation

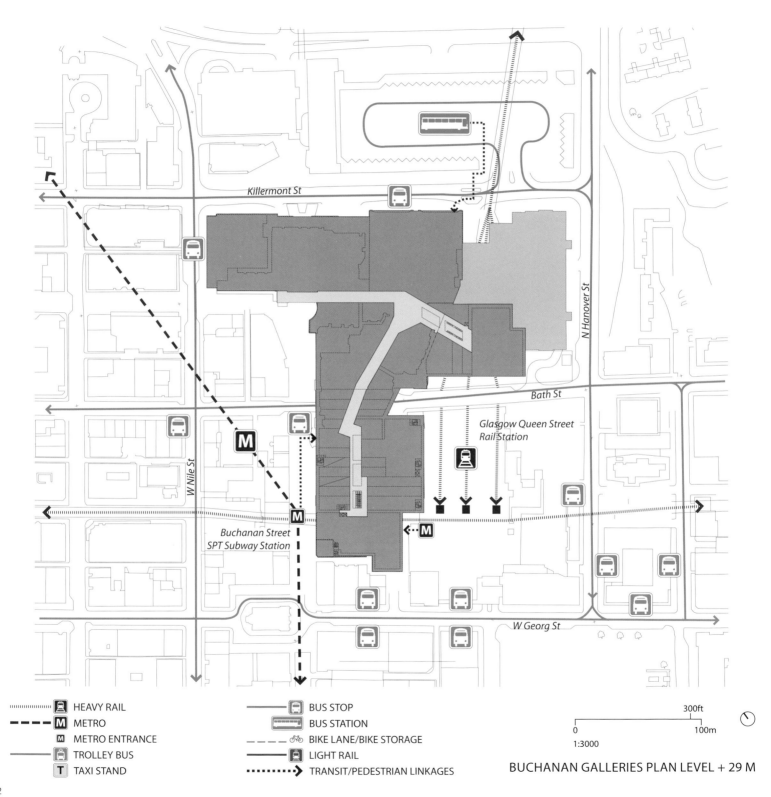

Killermont St

N Hanover St

Bath St

Glasgow Queen Street
Rail Station

W Nile St

M

M

Buchanan Street
SPT Subway Station

M

W Georg St

HEAVY RAIL

M METRO

M METRO ENTRANCE

TROLLEY BUS

T TAXI STAND

BUS STOP

BUS STATION

BIKE LANE/BIKE STORAGE

LIGHT RAIL

TRANSIT/PEDESTRIAN LINKAGES

300ft

0   100m

1:3000

BUCHANAN GALLERIES PLAN LEVEL + 29 M

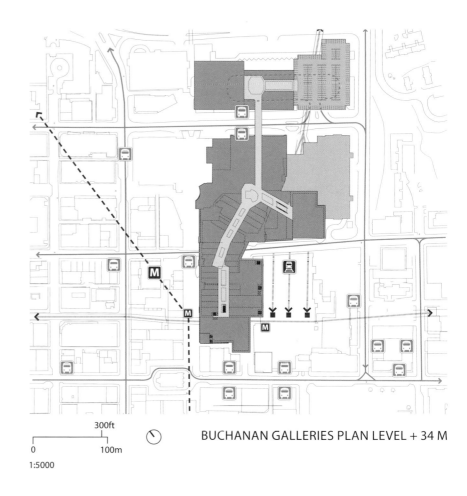

300ft

0   100m

1:5000

BUCHANAN GALLERIES PLAN LEVEL + 34 M

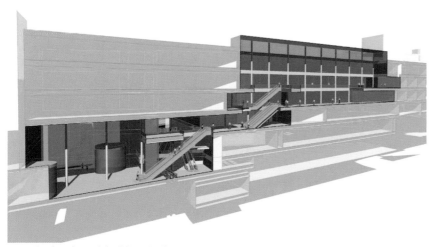

Section through building circulation

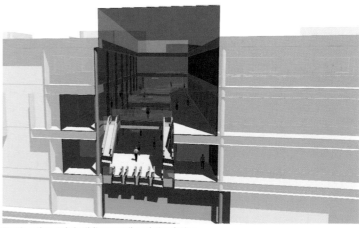

Section through building retail and circulation

TRANSIT ENVIRONMENT DEVELOPMENT

Transit Environment Development

A Transit Environment District (TED) describes a development area that is altered in some measurable fashion due to the convenience of being located within walking distance of a transit station. Significant alterations might include greater than normal density, fewer than required parking stalls, additional bicycle storage, services that are only possible as a consequence of the transit nearby, or unusual or special design that is made possible because of ready accessibility of a transit station.

Conveniently located pedestrian access points ensure easy passage to and from public transit. Additional bicycle access lanes and parking stalls are added.

The examples shown in this chapter are located in Australia and Eastern, Central and Western Europe.

Brno Campus Square

Brno, Czech Republic

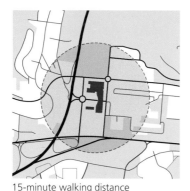

15-minute walking distance

Public Sector Needs

Established in 1869, the Brno transit network evolved into an extensive infrastructure connecting the various city districts. Transit zones were often dictated by master plans, and implemented prior to development. The purpose of Brno Campus Square was to complement the expansion of Masaryk University campus, Masaryk Hospital and City Archives, and act as a key element enabling the transit infrastructure of the local district to reach its full capacity, property value, and community benefit potential.

Private Sector Needs

From a development standpoint, the project had the potential to become an active gateway, and a community focal point for the new district. The project would build on the synergies among a new R&D office park, the Masaryk University campus, and the Brno University hospital. Development requirements included the realization of the campus expansion plans, and improvements to the pedestrian connection to the existing bus and trolley-bus terminal, adjacent to the project.

Project Issues

Critical transit-related issues included preserving a sloping city roadway running through the site, which could potentially damage the development's commercial viability; incorporating a public transit station on the other side of the busy road flanking the site, which was a barrier to pedestrian flow; and the potential problems caused by a bridge over the road connecting the campus activity level with the upper ground level of the project.

Design Solutions

The project design recognizes active edges at two different levels of the project: the upper access level, as approached from the highway; and the lower street level, where the trolley bus station and the hospital are located. The upper level coincides with the adjacent office development and elevated public pathways of the university campus, which are connected to the project by a pedestrian bridge. The lower street level activates the façade facing the bus terminal, with retail frontage and access to the level above through a community dining facility. The public road, which splits the site, is bridged by the upper level, allowing improved customer flow at the upper level. The new 269,000-square-foot (25,000-square-

Canopy provides clear, visual identity

meter) town center provides a two-level, open-air and enclosed shopping environment that includes a hypermarket, lifestyle and fashion retailers, as well as dining facilities. A large canopy provides a clear, visual identity for the new town center.

Public Benefits

The project serves as the gateway and community hub for the institutional, commercial, cultural and educational facilities that define the new Campus

District of Brno. The transit infrastructure is incorporated into the project in such a way as to create ease of access to the commercial part of the project, either by car via the ring road, or from the heart of Brno's city center via its transit system.

View from trolley bus station

Retail bridging above the public road

138

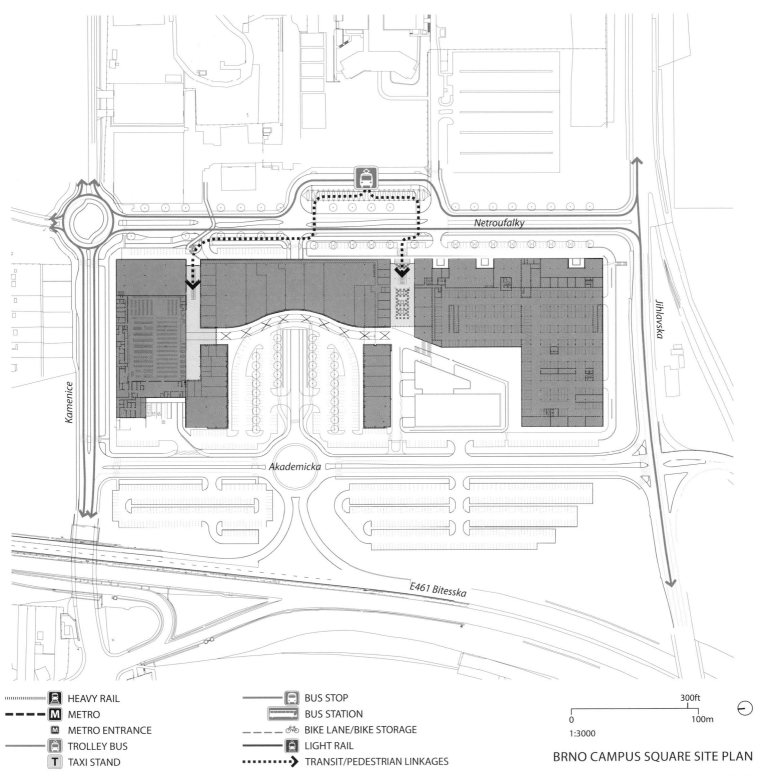

Kamenice

Netroufalky

Jihlavska

Akademicka

E461 Bitesska

300ft

0   100m

1:3000

BRNO CAMPUS SQUARE SITE PLAN

Mozaika (Third Ring)

Moscow, Russia

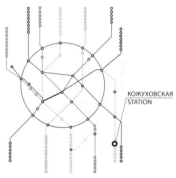

Moscow metro

15-minute walking distance

Public Sector Needs

The Third Ring highway encircling Moscow delivers drivers from across the city to prominent locations along it, including Mozaika. The project is also served by metro, streetcar and bus transit systems. The City Planning office, concerned by traffic impacts, sought a project that would encourage use of public transit, and mitigate the increase in traffic resulting from its construction.

Private Sector Needs

The developers, Simon Ivanhoe and OST Group, faced with significant planning and zoning restrictions, wanted to maximize the potential of the site, yet create a project that was easy to access and navigate. They sought a state-of-the-art design that would suit the neighborhood and put a positive face on the Third Ring.

Project Issues

To construct the project on a brownfield site, significant toxic soil needed to be removed, which would create a depressed site beneath the retail center. The existing one-way traffic street would necessarily impair access to and egress from the site by causing multiple left turns from a single point of arrival. The prospect of heavy frequency of overland truck stacking posed a challenge for vehicle and pedestrian access as well.

Design Solutions

Placing the primary retail level at street grade created convenient direct access for pedestrians arriving from the metro, tram and buses. A more liberal interpretation of the building code for parking on grade beneath the retail center resulted in 29 percent additional leasable area, creating a better draw for customers, and higher anticipated ridership on public transit. Traffic direction on the one-way street was reversed to allow for the free flow of traffic from the highway to the site, and out of the site back onto the highway. The design of a truck stacking area ensures the free flow of vehicular traffic, and the elimination of truck/pedestrian conflicts for those utilizing public transit.

Public Benefits

From a transit viewpoint, the project encourages the use of public transport, while reducing conflicts between the various vehicular uses. The convenience of locating the project on this particular site encourages the reduction of longer vehicle trips to more remote locations in other regional locations.

Aerial view

View from local avenue

Interior mall

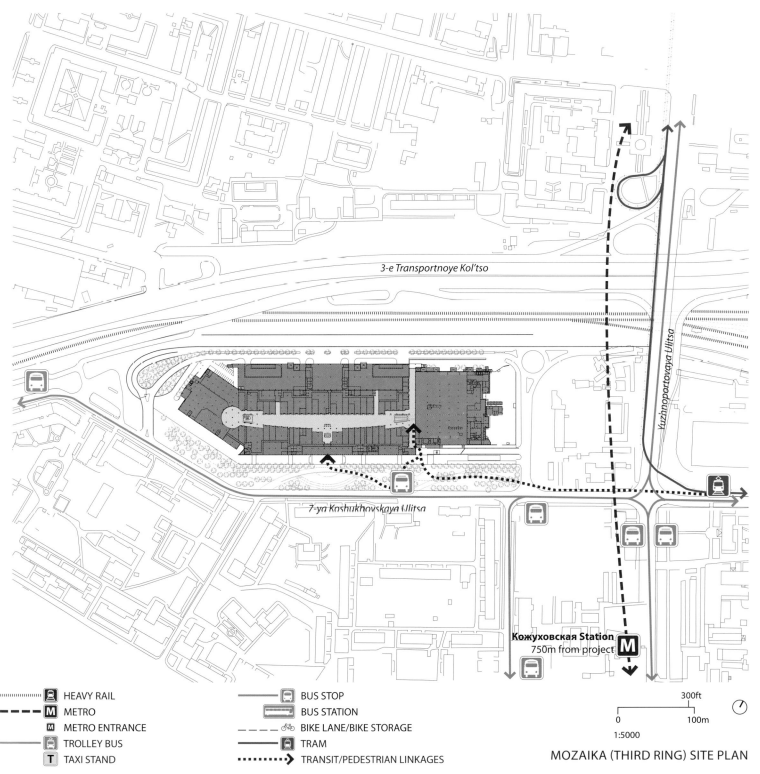

3-e Transportnoye Kol'tso

Yuzhnoportovaya Ulitsa

7-ya Koshukhovskaya Ulitsa

Кожуховская Station
750m from project **M**

	HEAVY RAIL		BUS STOP
M	METRO		BUS STATION
M	METRO ENTRANCE		BIKE LANE/BIKE STORAGE
	TROLLEY BUS		TRAM
T	TAXI STAND		TRANSIT/PEDESTRIAN LINKAGES

300ft

0   100m

1:5000

MOZAIKA (THIRD RING) SITE PLAN

Monash Village Caulfield Campus

Melbourne, Australia

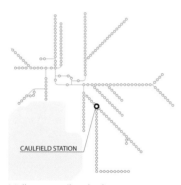

Melbourne rail and subway

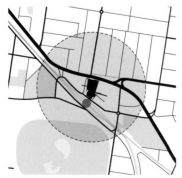

15-minute walking distance

Public Sector Needs

Monash University – Caulfield Campus is well-located on the periphery of Melbourne. It has a student population of over 13,000, and is easily accessible via mass transit or the Princes Highway. The campus had valuable land with substantial development potential, and the need to expand both its academic and commercial elements, but the university lacked the funds to realize these developments. The community of Glen Eira/Caulfield, where the university is located, had an existing high street adjacent to the campus, but the entities lacked interconnectivity.

Private Sector Needs

Private funding, construction and management of on-campus projects had potential benefits for all parties; however, the university and the municipality needed a series of agreements to make it happen. These included allowable development density, land values, infrastructure capacities, funding and financing instruments, rents/purchases, fees, and the timing of deliverables.

Project Issues

Critical issues involving potential development sites included occupancy by commercial tenants with existing leases, access points to and from the site, connections to the campus, high street and transit, and existing road capacities.

Design Solutions

As a public–private partnership, the project embraces the idea that university campuses can be a successful part of a high street atmosphere served by transit. Retail, student housing, classrooms and offices over two basement levels and six buildings are connected to the traditional streetscape as well as a campus green. Existing tenants became important stakeholders, and were provided with new and improved facilities. Connectivity to the development is achieved by a series of paths and civic spaces that act as focal points for people arriving by train, tram, bus, bike, or car. There is a casual, but effective, relationship created by the placement of buildings defining public space that encourages the use of three forms of public transit.

Mixed-use urban context

Public Benefits

The dedicated master plan became an instrument to realize the ambitions and visions of the university, the city, tenants, and developer/investors alike. The public benefits were such that the campus and the community went from isolated, independent worlds to an interconnected, highly accessible community appropriate for a city with one of the most comprehensive transit systems in the world.

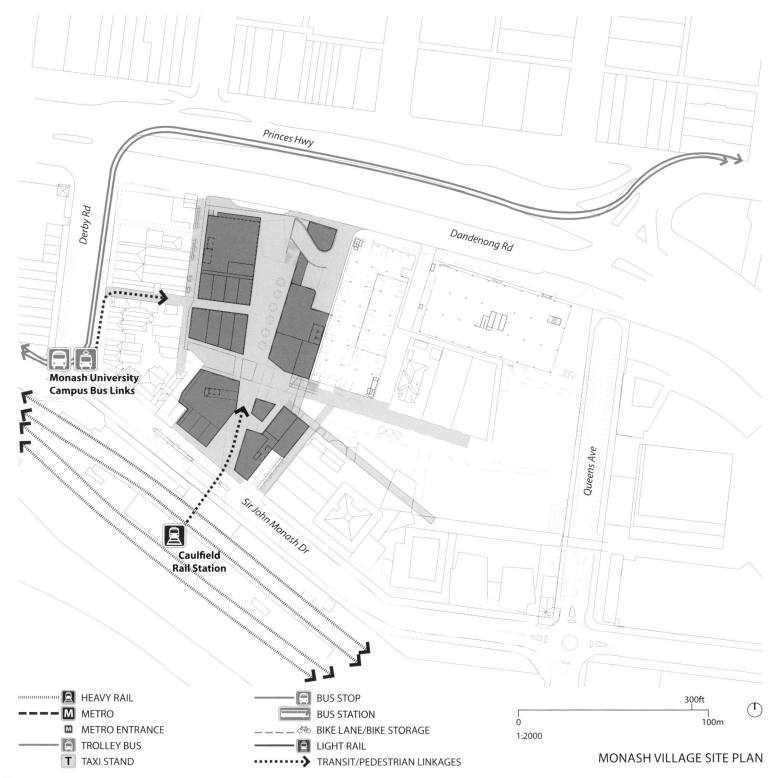

HEAVY RAIL

M METRO

M METRO ENTRANCE

TROLLEY BUS

T TAXI STAND

BUS STOP

BUS STATION

BIKE LANE/BIKE STORAGE

LIGHT RAIL

TRANSIT/PEDESTRIAN LINKAGES

300ft

0

100m

1:2000

MONASH VILLAGE SITE PLAN

View from Dandenong Road

Connectivity in a series of paths and civic spaces

Connectivity in a series of paths and civic spaces

The LOOP

Ghent, Belgium

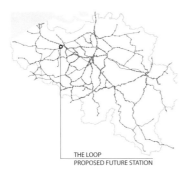

Belgium rail

THE LOOP
PROPOSED FUTURE STATION

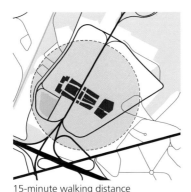

15-minute walking distance

Public Sector Needs

In order to accommodate responsible urban expansion, the City of Ghent established a new, master planned, mixed-use community. Funding and leadership for the development requires private investment, including Public Private Partnerships. As part of the master plan, The LOOP responds programmatically to City needs and potential with a mixed-use development energized by an outlet retail/leisure environment, offices and short-stay accommodation. One of the largest cities in Belgium, Ghent has a highly developed transportation system with significant expansion of the tram network being planned. The actual city center is a car-free area, and parking can be difficult.

Private Sector Needs

The LOOP offers potential profit and sustained benefits for private sector parties through a Public Private Partnership. Private sector needs include the creation of a mutually beneficial working relationship with the City of Ghent and adjacent property owners. Additionally, the private sector seeks approved adaptations to the City master plan in response to changes in property development and commercial tenant viabilities. Finally, the developers have asked the City to provide the infrastructure for parking, transit, roadways, bridges, and other engineering works.

Project Issues

The LOOP is situated adjacent to mass transit facilities, and at the intersection of two European transportation arteries. Critical transit issues relate to the incorporation of the planned extension of the tram and roadwork systems into the new town center. Challenges include minimizing conflicts between tram traffic, pedestrians, cyclists, automobiles, and service trucks and connecting the project with the adjacent Flanders Expo and a newly built IKEA.

Design Solutions

As The LOOP is envisioned to be a new urban district of Ghent, the design solutions for the project are founded in a marriage of landscape, urban fabric and community similar to the historic city. Formed by a contemporary collection of buildings, streets, and public spaces, The LOOP is a bridging urban entity in the landscape. This design solution overcomes the potentially divisive nature of the site's road networks by positioning the public realm above parking facilities, thereby allowing the project to span over the road. Because of the tram network, The Loop is a gateway to and from the historic city center of Ghent.

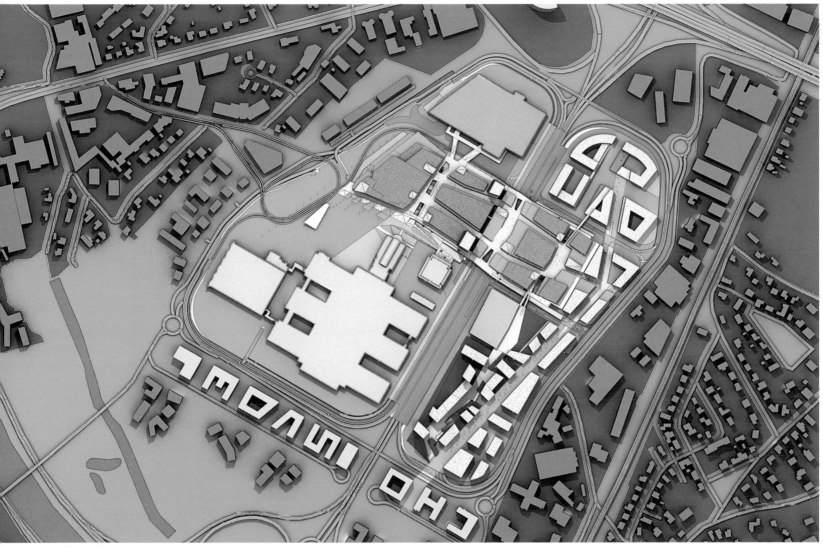

Bird's eye view

The LOOP is a portal to the inner city that provides a much needed park 'n' ride system, with parking for 5000 cars, tethered to the city center by tram networks. These parking facilities will be operated by city parking agencies and provide direct public sector revenue needs. The project connects to the existing tram system, and is designed to accommodate an extension of the rail system.

Public Benefits

With a heritage that is rich in culture, education, and commerce, Ghent has remained a vital urban environment for centuries. The LOOP speaks to the legacy of the community's inventive spirit by offering public benefits that include the development of a new urban district incorporating expansion of the city's tram network and the creation of much needed new parking spaces and subsequent revenue. In addition, the project creates a new European commercial and tourist attraction that will strengthen competitiveness in the marketplace.

Pedestrian paths exist above transit routes on street level

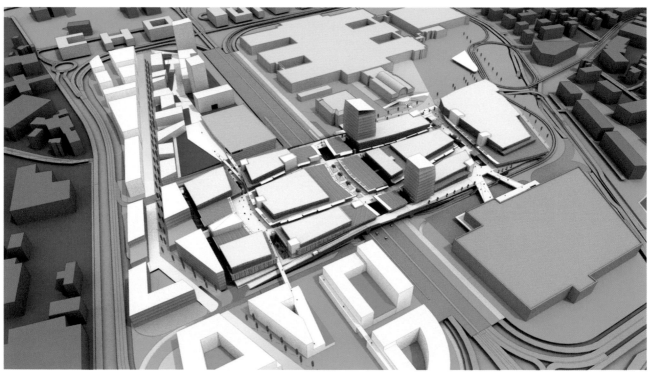

Aerial view

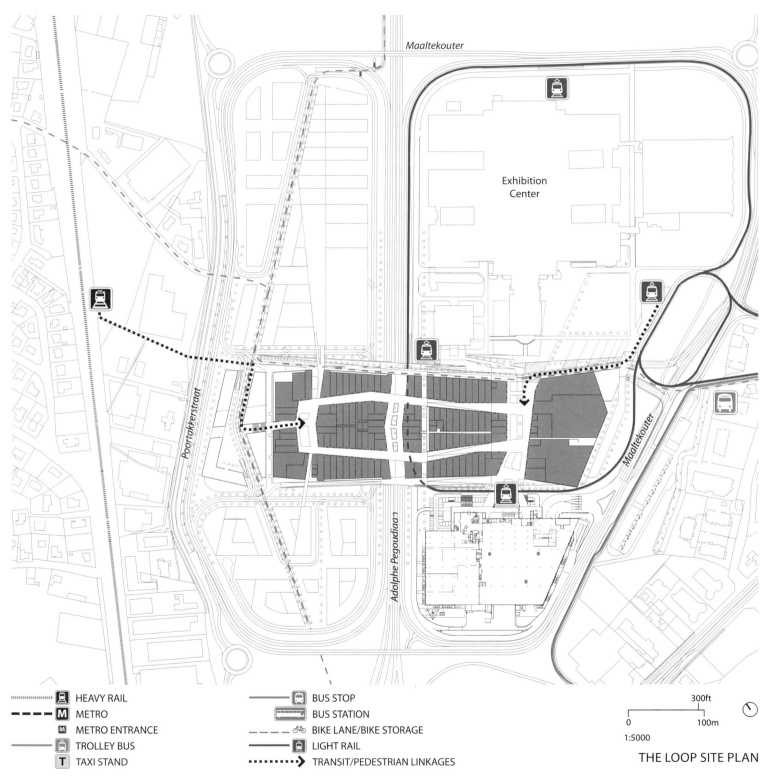

Exhibition
Center

Maaltekouter

Poortakkerstraat

Adolphe Pegoudlaan

Maaltekouter

	HEAVY RAIL		BUS STOP
	METRO		BUS STATION
	METRO ENTRANCE		BIKE LANE/BIKE STORAGE
	TROLLEY BUS		LIGHT RAIL
T	TAXI STAND		TRANSIT/PEDESTRIAN LINKAGES

300ft

0   100m

1:5000

THE LOOP SITE PLAN

Daming Palace National Heritage Park Development
Xi'an, China

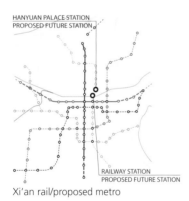

Xi'an rail/proposed metro

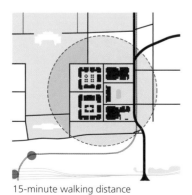

15-minute walking distance

Public Sector Needs

Daming Palace was the home of the first Emperor of united China, known for his tomb of terra-cotta soldiers. His palace, recently conserved, is now a national landmark. The Daming Palace retail center site sits adjacent to, and at the point of arrival to, this historic site, across the street from the central railroad station. The public sector sought a project that would engage visitors transiting from the train to the palace, in a manner that would be respectful of this unique cultural treasure. The street grid, which had been overlaid onto the site in the early 20th century, was to be incorporated into the scheme. In addition, one historic structure and a public school, centrally located within the boundaries of the development site, were to remain in place.

Private Sector Needs

The developer, Xi'an Qujiang Daming Palace Investment Group, Ltd., wanted a project sufficiently porous so as to allow unfettered access from all sides in a natural and comfortable manner. The vehicular street system needed to be utilized not as a divider of blocks, but as a connector for pedestrians within the overall composition—no easy task in a tourist-oriented venue. With an unusual program designed not only for tourist interests, but also the local market for fashion, food, banqueting, and entertainment, the challenges were significant. Servicing needed to be handled in a discrete manner.

Project Issues

While rectangular in shape, the site was located on a gentle incline, and divided by the street grid into five dissimilar sizes. The historic building could be adaptively reused as a part of the overall commercial complex, but the school needed to be isolated from the public functions of the retail center. The conflicting relationship between pedestrian and vehicular traffic needed resolution. The project also needed to engage the transit station.

Design Solutions

The project design follows the building principles of historic Chinese courtyards. Two-story building masses surround courtyards in which additional pavilions are placed, reducing the overall scale of the buildings and that of the internal spaces. Formal and axial in composition, they create a "maze" of experiences that begin at the point of axis of the palace entry great forecourt, which, in turn, leads axially to the heart of the Daming Palace itself. More importantly, it is designed to provide multiple points of access for pedestrians utilizing the existing railroad and proposed two subway stops, all contiguous to the development.

Aerial view

Public Benefits

Housing traditional Chinese arts, crafts and culinary choices, as well as other retail and entertainment offers, the Daming Palace Retail Cultural Complex will provide a transitional experience, from the realities of the city to the tranquility of the ancient past. It complements the historic destination with a 21st-century facility that provides a fuller appreciation of the historic context, thereby encouraging the use of public transit to access the dual experience. When a planned museum is completed opposite the grand forecourt, the transit draw will further increase.

Street system serves as a connector for pedestrians

Courtyard design

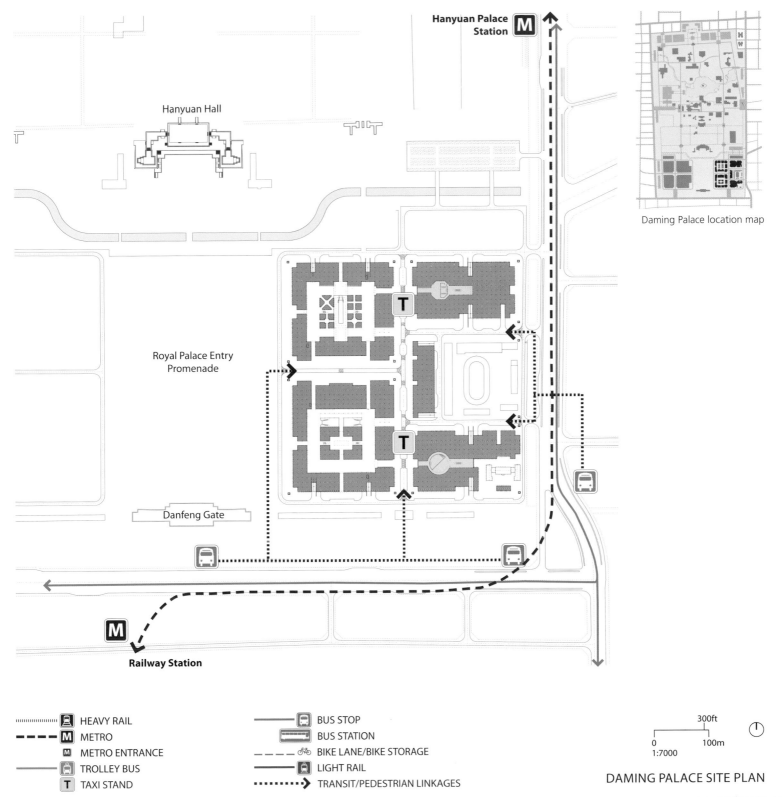

Hanyuan Palace
Station **M**

Hanyuan Hall

Daming Palace location map

Royal Palace Entry
Promenade

T

T

Danfeng Gate

M

Railway Station

300ft

0   100m
1:7000

DAMING PALACE SITE PLAN

TRANSIT INDUCING DEVELOPMENT

Transit Inducing Development

A Transit Inducing Development (TID) project, inspired by the pending arrival of public transit, may influence the location of a transit station box or station portals. Such projects can affect the transit station itself, sometimes in ways not envisioned by the transit agency. Indeed, the integration of transit into the project may encourage more reciprocal engagement between the transit rider and the development.

These projects have not previously been considered part of the TOD realm because they precede the formal planning of transit integration with conventional development. However, they bring great value as catalyst projects. One example is located adjacent to an historic railroad station, but envisions the relocation of a light rail line, bus station and taxi stand. It caused the transit agencies to reconsider their alignment and the geometrics of operations of their respective facilities. A second was designed for a developer in parallel with the alignment selection by the transit agency to best facilitate both interests.

The resulting projects would be designated as TOD or TAD projects when completed. One is located in Europe, and the other in the United States.

Charleroi Station Hub Master Plan

Brussels, Belgium

CHARLEROI-SUD
STATION

Belgium rail

15-minute walking distance

Public Sector Needs

The City of Charleroi, a community 30 miles (48 kilometers) outside Brussels, serves as a southern gateway to and from France. The historic railroad station, which sits south of the downtown area on the side of a working canal, delivers riders to a local bus and tram system that occupies land in a former plaza directly in front of the station, significantly impairing its image. The City needed to establish connectivity between the station and the historic city core, and sought a major investment in the form of real estate development to encourage a much-needed economic revitalization. At the same time, the community wished to protect the low scale, incremental texture of its city form and building massing, while accommodating a better conceived, more efficient transit hub.

Private Sector Needs

The developer, Equilis, was faced with the daunting task of resolving transit interface logistics and city planning parameters. They also needed to accommodate office, retail, hotel, entertainment, dining and civic uses on the long, narrow, compressed site, which only had one point of access. Given the expensive financial hurdles of relocating transit uses and the adaptive reuse of an unattractive former post office structure, the development had to be very efficient and appealing to win customer acceptance.

Project Issues

The site was constrained by railroad tracks on the long south edge, a canal on the north, a highway to the west, and a busy intersection on the east, with the only available access off a narrow roadway running parallel to the canal. Poor pedestrian connections from the site to the core of the historic downtown were in need of redesign for comfort and convenience. Vehicular access for park 'n' ride customers needed to be isolated from access for commercial visitors and hotel guests. Competing transit agencies were not eager to discuss mutually beneficial solutions, thereby favoring the status quo and posing additional challenges to good planning, design and civic use.

Design Solutions

In order for planning to proceed, an optimal solution for the light rail and bus station interface was required, which would allow for the integration of a taxi stand into the design. Additional pedestrian bridges would connect various aspects of the program to the core of the historic city. The resulting scheme acknowledges that the civic use—the railroad station—merited a

Perspective showing taxi queue along canal

civic space, and that all other functions—light rail, bus, taxi, retail, dining and entertainment—could be accessed directly from the formal gathering space, which in turn would link directly into the town square located a short walk across the axial bridge.

Public Benefits

The design vision creates a civic focus for Charleroi, with a city portal worthy of the community and its position as a gateway to Belgium from France. Moreover, the project provides a mixed-use, soft-scaled development.

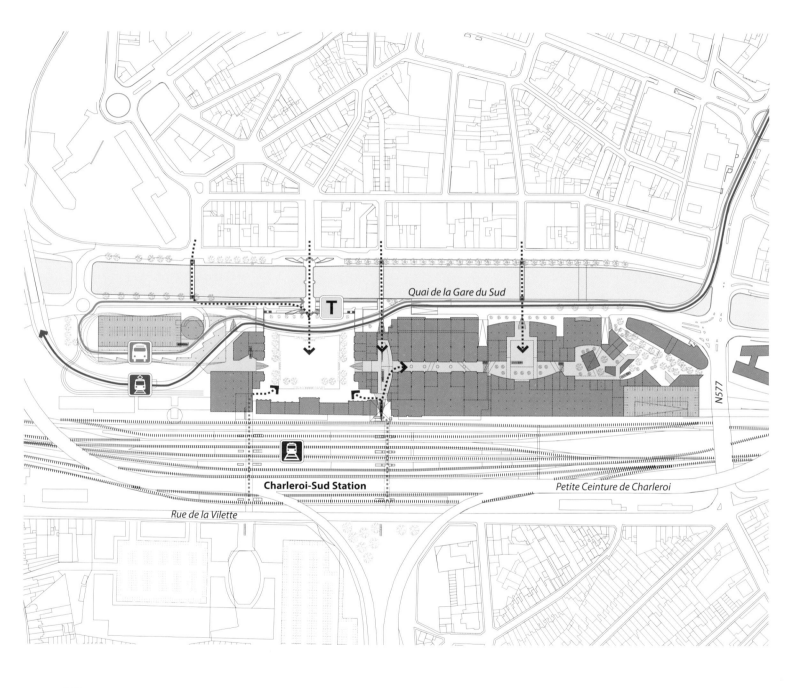

Quai de la Gare du Sud

T

N577

Charleroi-Sud Station

Petite Ceinture de Charleroi

Rue de la Vilette

⸽⸽⸽ 🚆	HEAVY RAIL	── 🚌	BUS STOP	
─ ─ M	METRO	▭	BUS STATION	
M	METRO ENTRANCE	─ ─ 🚲	BIKE LANE/BIKE STORAGE	
─ 🚋	TROLLEY BUS	── 🚈	LIGHT RAIL	
T	TAXI STAND	▪▪▪▪▶	TRANSIT/PEDESTRIAN LINKAGES	

300ft

0   100m

1:4000

CHARLEROI SITE PLAN

New civic space

Pedestrian bridges link the station hub to the core of the historic city

Fashion Valley Center

San Diego, California

San Diego light rail

15-minute walking distance

Public Sector Needs

In expanding its light rail option for rapid rail transit across the region, San Diego's Metropolitan Transit System pursued the use of at-grade or elevated solutions, using readily available, reliable, and scalable technologies that would take advantage of transportation or public rights-of-way where possible, and would link to development and other modes of transit. Cost was a motivating factor, since financial viability is a consistent issue for transit agencies. The opportunity to locate a station at an operating shopping center was deemed a sound decision.

Private Sector Needs

From the developer's perspective, accepting the location of the trolley station along with the kiss 'n' ride, park 'n' ride, and bus terminal on their retail center site expedited the approval of the proposed renovations and additions to Fashion Valley which had begun in the late 1980s and ran until the early 1990s. The incorporation of the station as well as the specific design proposals helped to assuage concerns that shoppers would not have alternative transit options in traveling to the center.

Project Issues

While there was adequate land to accommodate the station, the ground level area of the site was prone to flooding, especially in a major storm. In addition, there were concerns about stacking buses, and the area needed to effect transfer of customers across modes of transit.

Design Solutions

By locating the light rail platform for the trolley at the proposed second level of the Fashion Valley expansion, at the side of the shopping center adjacent to the San Diego River right-of-way and directly over the proposed regional bus terminal, the design allowed for significant bus and passenger vehicle stacking distance into and out of the site. In turn, the stacking distance and station location allowed for easy movement of all modes of transportation on and off the site, without complicating local street traffic.

The location of the trolley platform and access bridge also provided improved pedestrian access to the shopping center, in an area that benefitted from the increased foot traffic. The new parking structures were located in a lower level area, which helped with flood control and storm water detention in Mission Valley during major storms, and provide direct access to the ground level platform.

Trolley platform

Fashion Valley Transit Center bus terminal

Aerial view of Fashion Valley and Transit Center

Public Benefits

While there is always concern about how adding square footage, parking and transit will create problems, even with the increase of shopping center area, additional parking and the bus and rail stations, traffic has stabilized. Importantly, revenue is up and ridership on all modes of transit continues to increase.

The ongoing success of the center is a benefit to the city as a shopping destination for tourists as well as locals, which increases sales tax revenues. Moreover, the thoughtful planning and location of the station anticipated future growth, with room to accommodate greater densities and a mix of complementary uses over time.

New second level

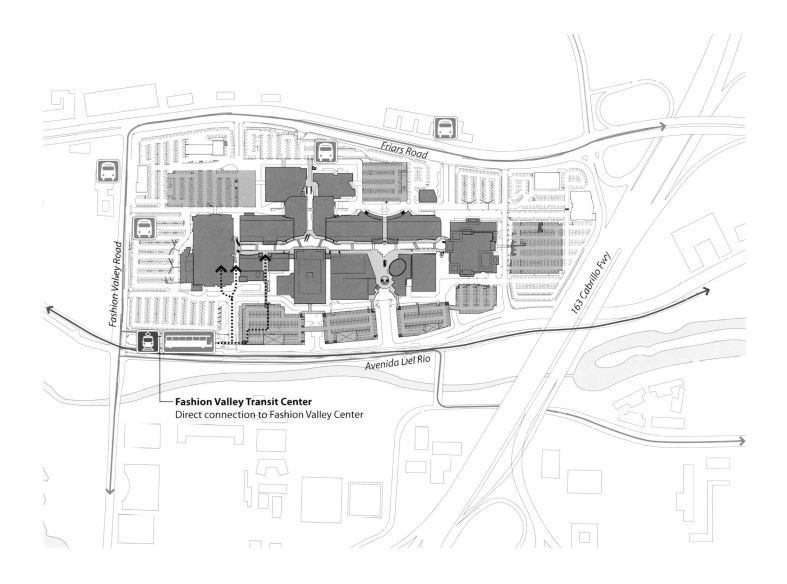

Fashion Valley Transit Center
Direct connection to Fashion Valley Center

Friars Road

Fashion Valley Road

163 Cabrillo Fwy

Avenida Del Rio

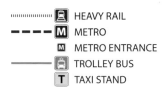

	HEAVY RAIL
M	METRO
M	METRO ENTRANCE
	TROLLEY BUS
T	TAXI STAND

	BUS STOP
	BUS STATION
	BIKE LANE/BIKE STORAGE
	LIGHT RAIL
·····>	TRANSIT/PEDESTRIAN LINKAGES

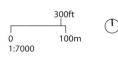

300ft

0   100m
1:7000

FASHION VALLEY CENTER SITE PLAN

DEVELOPMENT INDUCING TRANSIT

Development Inducing Transit

Although there are few examples where the design of a development project envisions a public benefit not currently defined by the public sector—a Development Inducing Transit (DIT)—those rare exceptions hold great value as prototypes. Such a project has the ability to induce transit stations to be constructed in locations that have not as yet been identified by the transit authorities. They may be designed to accept a potential transit box and/or station that has been discussed, but not budgeted, or the private sector developers might propose that, in the public interest, a station be considered in the future. Two projects have been selected as examples to illustrate these two possibilities.

The first is designed to accommodate a direct linkage to a transit station box that has not been funded or constructed although a station has been discussed as an objective. Accordingly, the project was designed to encourage the line to be extended to the subject site. The other project, fronting a long, industrial rail line, was designed in recognition that it would soon be obsolete for commercial use, and could be re-envisioned to serve a commuter base. With a strong connection to a multi-modal station, a destination would be established that could yield a TAD project after the fact.

The two examples depicted are from Asia and the United States.

Marina City

Qingdao, China

Future Qingdao metro

15-minute walking distance

Public Sector Needs

The 2008 Beijing Olympics created a flurry of construction activity throughout China, particularly on sites close to sports venues. At the Qingdao waterfront—the location for the Olympic sailing events—Marina City occupied a site immediately adjacent to the sailing craft harbor. The site featured a broad ocean front promenade straddling both sides of the International Avenue of Flags, on axis with the central business district. An underground subway station was planned to deliver spectators from the city to the axial avenue located between the east and west parcels of the property. In addition, bus services would drop patrons off directly next to the site. The government agencies sought a project that would not only serve as a destination for transit riders, but would also be a world-class gateway to Qingdao for Olympic spectators.

Private Sector Needs

In order to accommodate the Avenue of Flags, the developer, Qingdao Tai Shan Real Estate Co. Ltd, was faced with a bifurcated project freighted with multiple demands for design attention—serving as an Olympics-worthy portal and civic space, creating a focus on the waterfront, and effecting urban connectivity. The desire for a cohesive, mixed-use development—retail, leisure, entertainment, dining, office, service apartments and civic space—posed a significant challenge, particularly when coupled with site issues.

Project Issues

The large, rectangular site, adjacent to the ocean, had a very high water table that posed critical engineering challenges. The Avenue divided the parcel into two distinct components—the East Village, an enclosed three-level fashion gallery; and the West Village, a two-level open air lifestyle complex—that were connected below grade by a retail, dining and leisure concourse. The location, adjacent to other new developments, posed linkage challenges as well. A proposed subway transit connection was not yet specifically determined, but it was clear to the planning authorities that the portals would be on the north end of the Avenue of Flags, between the East and West Village. Bus stops were to be located along the northern facade.

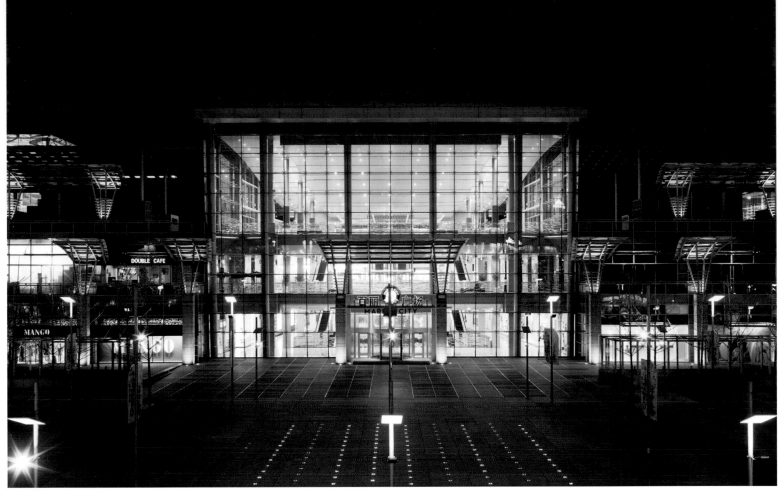

East Village entrance off Avenue of the Flags plaza

Design Solutions

The project was designed to bookend and focus attention on the major civic space on the Avenue of Flags. There, customers coming and going through the transit portal had direct access to the Olympic site, the civic space, and the primary entrances of both retail/mixed-use villages.

Public Benefits

When the transit agency completed the station portals adjacent to Marina City, the measurable, long-term benefits of the public–private interface became evident. Not only is the Olympic venue permanently accessible for tourists and the regional community, but the project's high quality commercial offerings are readily available for the immediate neighborhood. While civic spaces are rarely found in conjunction with private development, the project begins with a sense of civic obligation which is at the heart of the development. The transit linkage makes it available region-wide.

Aerial view

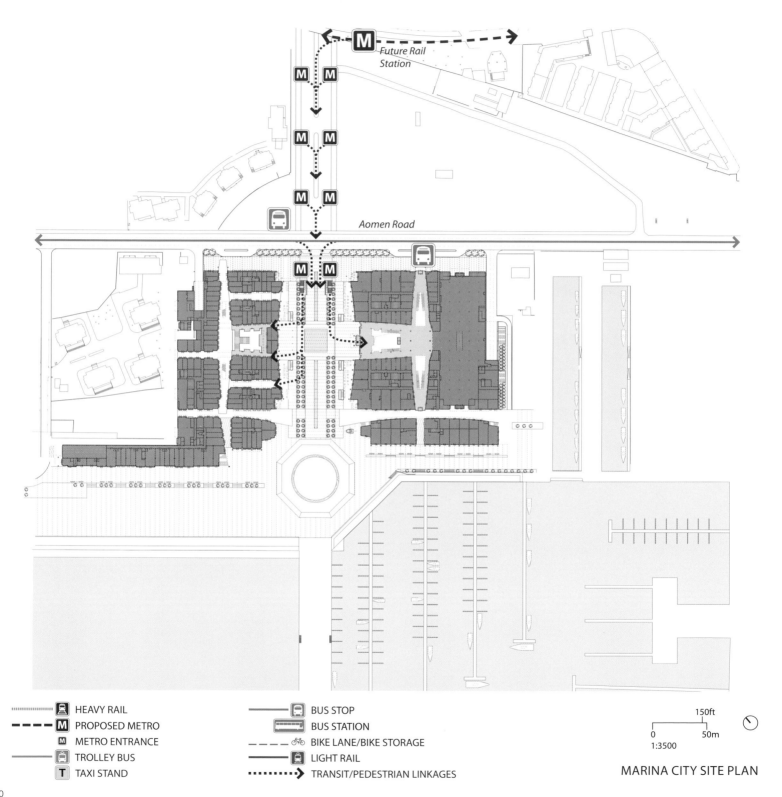

Future Rail Station

Aomen Road

	HEAVY RAIL		BUS STOP
	PROPOSED METRO		BUS STATION
	METRO ENTRANCE		BIKE LANE/BIKE STORAGE
	TROLLEY BUS		LIGHT RAIL
	TAXI STAND		TRANSIT/PEDESTRIAN LINKAGES

150ft

0   50m

1:3500

MARINA CITY SITE PLAN

West Village

Marina City station portals in Avenue of Flags plaza

East Village entrance off Aomen Road

172

Interior mall

Redmond Town Center

Redmond, Washington

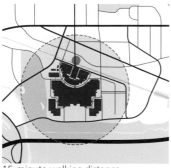

15-minute walking distance

Public Sector Needs

Redmond, a suburban community located about eight minutes east of downtown Seattle, is home to Microsoft. At the time the project was planned, there were no public transit options for this growth area, except for a park 'n' ride and kiss 'n' ride bus station, located at the intersection of the southern end of the major north–south avenue and an industrial railroad track alignment. The rail allowed two local industries to be serviced directly from the tracks. One, a dairy, was scheduled to close within a year. The other, directly across the street from the bus station and the project site, was a feed store whose sales were decreasing as livestock businesses relocated further west. The public sector needed, but had not envisioned, a light rail linkage into the heart of Seattle, serving all the communities along the route.

Private Sector Needs

Winmar, the developer of Redmond Town Center, had plans for a major mixed-use project, which would include a regional shopping center, two office buildings, a business hotel, entertainment uses, and a town square acting as the terminus of the north–south avenue. With the park 'n' ride facility just across the tracks from the site, the community and private sector would benefit from more efficient public transit, and transit choices, which would link the project to surrounding areas and strengthen its appeal.

Project Issues

Major projects should not be considered only in the context of present conditions, but as catalysts to inspire change. The proposed 1.4-million-square-foot (426,720-square-meter), mixed-use project had tremendous potential as a change agent for the community. While the feed store owners did not see relocation as an option, the designers understood that the potential impediment presented by the store along the rail tracks could be converted into an opportunity that would drive the development.

Aerial view

Design Solutions

The developer approached the City to consider relocating administrative functions to one of the proposed office buildings seeking a civic use to complement the program. The project design featured the major civic space, which became the focal point for the commercial and civic buildings, hotel, cinema, restaurants and regional shopping center, creating an urban destination and transit hub unparalleled in the entire Pacific Northwest region. With the creation of a compelling destination, the conversion of the existing transit site into a multi-modal station, and the relocation of the feed store offsite, the project provided the optimum conditions to convert the railroad right-of-way into a light rail line.

Public Benefits

Private sector vision in the public interest sometimes precedes that of the public sector. In situations such as this, development serves as a catalyst for the creation of transit lines and transit stations that encourage public transit ridership.

Entrance

Retail fronting the proposed new road

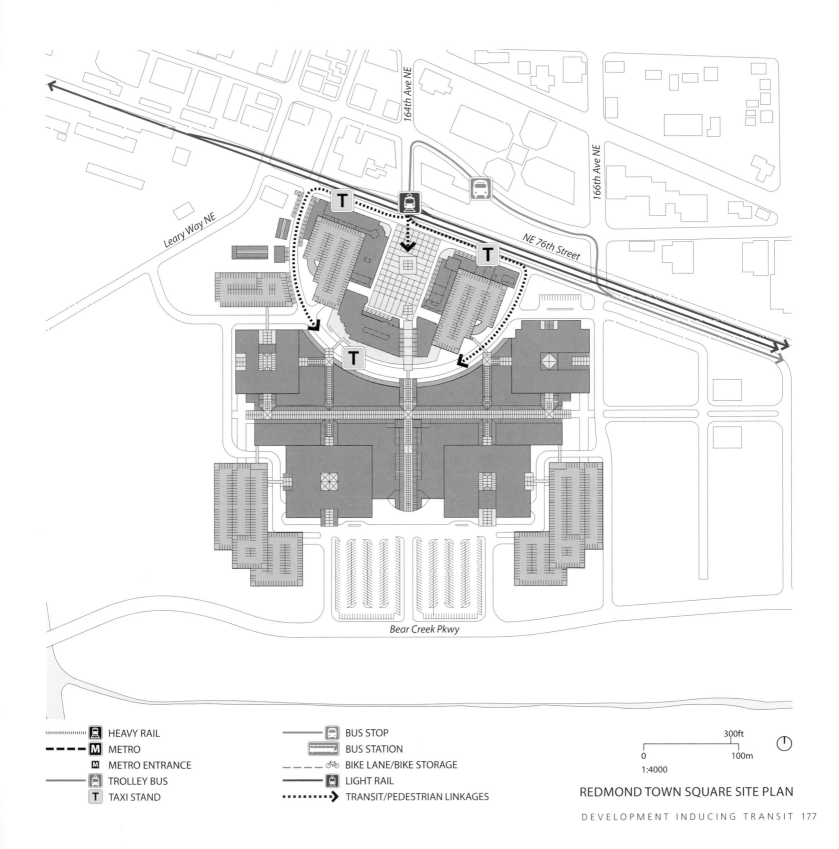

164th Ave NE

166th Ave NE

Leary Way NE

NE 76th Street

T

T

T

Bear Creek Pkwy

	HEAVY RAIL		BUS STOP
	METRO		BUS STATION
	METRO ENTRANCE		BIKE LANE/BIKE STORAGE
	TROLLEY BUS		LIGHT RAIL
	TAXI STAND		TRANSIT/PEDESTRIAN LINKAGES

300ft

0   100m

1:4000

REDMOND TOWN SQUARE SITE PLAN

CONCLUSION

Transit related development projects come in many stripes and spots. There is no absolute formula. Yet, the most successful projects begin with an envisioned outcome that delivers a public amenity without damaging the private sector, which assumes the financial risk. Civic in nature, such projects create a sense of destination. As importantly, they fulfill a social, cultural, recreational or economical purpose.

These developments are, in the end, the marriage of a public sector mandate—to create more livable and sustainable cities—and private sector vision— to realize successful real estate investments. At best, the relationship between these two forces is collaborative, rather than competitive or combative. These partnerships, often formalized by integrated investment strategies with clearly defined obligations into Public Private Partnerships, are proving to be the best means for all parties to achieve their objectives.

In studying the process and the best examples of TODs, several lessons learned emerge. First, it is critical that the public sector understand the risk assumed by the private sector partner and the return required to the secure financing. Investors expect a balance between good transportation policy and real estate disposition. Second, the private sector justifiably expects that public sector staff exercise a high degree of leadership, especially as the transit agency becomes the most influential force in dealing with the local governing agency. The developer expects the assistance of the transit agency in complying with the local municipality's planning department. The private sector cannot win an argument with a local municipality without transit agency support and leadership. Third, often, the scale and size of projects mandates a more comprehensive environmental analysis. Environmental Impact Reports are lengthy, costly, time consuming, and cannot be circumvented. Leadership—at every level of both the public sector and private sector—is essential.

Transit Oriented Development projects are not for the faint hearted. If it is necessary for a private sector developer and the team of architects, engineers, and other consultants to be experienced, world-class talents, then the public sector leadership and staff at all levels—federal, state, county and municipality—who have jurisdiction over any aspect of these projects, should also bring equivalent world-class skill sets. Without well-matched teams, with leadership and talent, on both sides of the table, the most worthy of projects has the potential to fail.

This leads to a discussion of process. First, it is important to begin with a mutually agreed upon set of goals. Some call this interest alignment. Second, it is critical to identify the professionals who are experienced, creative, flexible, and competent—in short, world class—to negotiate, support, advocate for, and implement the entire transaction, from concept to operation. Third, it is critical to identify leaders. Leaders, from both the public and private sector, articulate a vision and encourage others to embrace it, and they are willing to take risks. They know how to build world-class teams and secure the mandate to move forward aggressively.

TODs are very complicated projects to build. Most often, the transit system is operating during the entire construction process. Construction logistics translate to logistics in design and engineering, which, in turn, translate to logistics in development and negotiations between the public and private sectors, and logistics in neighborhood acceptance. Such complexity requires not only the capabilities, but also the disposition, to handle the inevitable, conflicting constraints in a synchronized fashion. These unconventional construction issues create challenges in identifying financing sources. Alternative financing strategies, such as Tax Increment Financing (TIF), allow a private sector developer to borrow against the future tax revenue generated by the investment, and the sale of municipal bonds. They may be utilized to finance infrastructure needs, such as park 'n' ride parking structures, and may help justify a development project investment that otherwise could not meet economic tests.

These examples, taken from Altoon + Porter's nearly three decades of global practice, are but a few of many others, currently in the design process. The sine curve is pointing steeply up, signaling the increased commitment by public and private entities, in both market driven and command economies, to focus attention on this critical element of the urban infrastructure.

In the 19th century, Napoleon III commissioned Baron Georges-Eugene Haussmann to create a modernization program to transform the medieval village pattern of Paris with a structure of boulevards, avenues and streets that created the present City of Light. The overlay of comprehensive public transit systems brings similar potential to our dysfunctional cities today. Beyond enhanced mobility comes the promise of a paradigm shift in the physical structure of cities—an evolution from single-use horizontal to mixed-use vertical zoning, from low to higher density, from congested traffic and polluted air to a healthy and sustainable environment. The 21st century appears destined to be the era when civilization got out of the car, on to the train, and learned to walk upright again.

APPENDIX

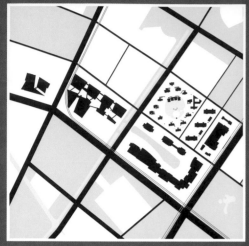

WALSIN CENTRO
NANJING, CHINA

SENGKANG MRT STATION
SINGAPORE

BUANGKOK MRT STATION
SINGAPORE

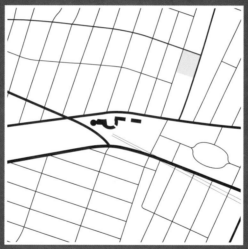

PICO/SAN VICENTE STATION
LOS ANGELES, CALIFORNIA

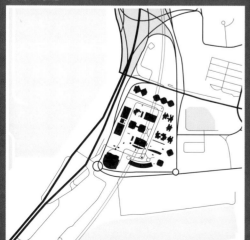

KOWLOON STATION
HONG KONG, CHINA

HOLLYWOOD & HIGHLAND
LOS ANGELES, CALIFORNIA

TORONTO UNION STATION
TORONTO, ONTARIO, CANADA

CENTRUM CHODOV
PRAGUE, CZECH REPUBLIC

METALLIST CITY CENTRE
KHARKIV, UKRAINE

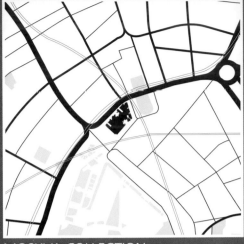

MOSKVA COLLECTION
MOSCOW, RUSSIA

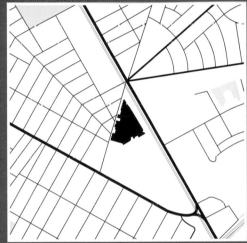

VICTORIA CITY
BUCHAREST, ROMANIA

MUCHA CENTRE
PRAGUE, CZECH REPUBLIC

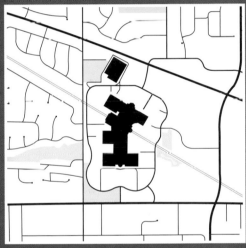

GRESHAM STATION
GRESHAM, OREGON

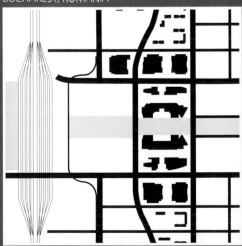

WALSIN MIXED-USE COMPLEX
JINAN, CHINA

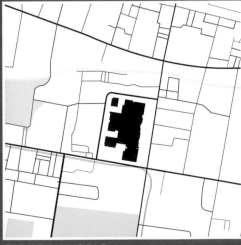

CENTRALWORLD
BANGKOK, THAILAND

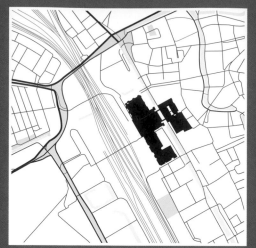

NIEUW HOOG CATHARIJNE
UTRECHT, THE NETHERLANDS

THE SHOPS AT TANFORAN
SAN BRUNO, CALIFORNIA

THE ATRIUM AT KURSKY SQUARE
MOSCOW, RUSSIA

YASENEVO
MOSCOW, RUSSIA

WUHAN SHIMAO CARNIVAL
WUHAN, CHINA

BUCHANAN GALLERIES
GLASGOW, SCOTLAND

BRNO CAMPUS SQUARE
BRNO, CZECH REPUBLIC

MOZAIKA (THIRD RING)
MOSCOW, RUSSIA

MONASH UNIVERSITY CAULFIELD
MELBOURNE, AUSTRALIA

THE LOOP
GHENT, BELGIUM

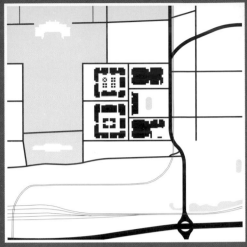

DAMING PALACE
XI'AN, CHINA

CHARLEROI STATION HUB
BRUSSELS, BELGIUM

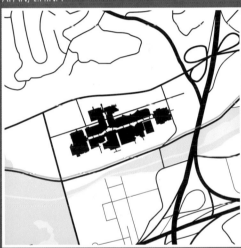

FASHION VALLEY CENTER
SAN DIEGO, CALIFORNIA

MARINA CITY
QINGDAO, CHINA

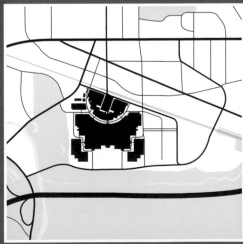

REDMOND TOWN CENTER
REDMOND, WASHINGTON

ALTOON + PORTER ARCHITECTS LLP
TRANSIT PROJECT TIME LINE

MULTI CASA CENTRAL STATION
DUISBURG, GERMANY

YASENEVO
MOSCOW, RUSSIA

KOWLOON STATION
HONG KONG, CHINA

UNION PARK
LEEDS, UNITED KINGDOM

MONASH VILLAGE CAULFIELD CAMPUS
MELBOURNE, AUSTRALIA

CENTRUM CHODOV
PRAGUE, CZECH REPUBLIC

FASHION VALLEY CENTER
SAN DIEGO, CALIFORNIA, USA

HOLLYWOOD & HIGHLAND
LOS ANGELES, CALIFORNIA, USA

BUCHANAN GALLERIES
GLASGOW, SCOTLAND, UK

THE SHOPS AT TANFORAN
SAN BRUNO, CALIFORNIA, USA

──────── BUILT
·············· COMPLETED DESIGN / UNBUILT

REDMOND TOWN CENTER
REDMOND, WASHINGTON, USA

GRESHAM STATION
GRESHAM, OREGON, USA

ONE WILSHIRE
LOS ANGELES, CALIFORNIA, USA

BROADWAY PLAZA
LOS ANGELES, CALIFORNIA, USA

MCA UNIVERSAL
LOS ANGELES, CALIFORNIA, USA

PICO/SAN VICENTE STATION
LOS ANGELES, CALIFORNIA, USA

SOUTHWESTERN UNIVERSITY SCHOOL OF LAW LIBRARY
LOS ANGELES, CALIFORNIA, USA

WARRINGAH MALL
BROOKVALE, SYDNEY, AUSTRALIA

MUCHA CENTRE
PRAGUE, CZECH REPUBLIC

GRAND AVENUE PLAN
LOS ANGELES, CALIFORNIA, USA

BOTANY TOWN CENTRE
AUCKLAND, NEW ZEALAND

THE ATRIUM AT KURSKY STATION
MOSCOW, RUSSIA

SENGKANG MRT STATION
SINGAPORE

BUANGKOK MRT STATION
SINGAPORE

| 1986 | 1989 | 1992 | 1993 | 1995 | 1996 | 1997 | 1998 | 1999 | 2000 | 2001 | 2002 | 2004 | 2005 |

2006

MARINA SQUARE
SINGAPORE

PACIFICENTER/DOUGLAS PARK
LONG BEACH, CALIFORNIA, USA

SHORELINE GATEWAY
LONG BEACH, CALIFORNIA, USA

ODINTSOVO MIXED-USE
MOSCOW, RUSSIA

2007

CENTRAL WORLD
BANGKOK, THAILAND

THE LOOP
GHENT, BELGIUM

WAIKIKI BEACH WALK
HONOLULU, HAWAI'I, USA

THE PORT - BRATISLAVA
BRATISLAVA, SLOVAKIA

2008

BRNO CAMPUS SQUARE
BRNO, CZECH REPUBLIC

CHARLEROI STATION HUB MASTER PLAN
BRUSSELS, BELGIUM

PARAMAZ AVEDISIAN BUILDING AMERICAN UNIV. OF ARMENIA
YEREVAN, ARMEN A

JAIDING CENTER
SHANGHAI, CHINA

COMMERCIAL COMPLEX
NIZHNIY NOVGOROD, RUSSIA

KRASNOGORSK MIXED-USE CENTER
KRASNOGORSK, RUSSIA

MOZAIKA (THIRD RING)
MOSCOW, RUSSIA

NOVOSIBIRSK
NOVOSIBIRSK, RUSSIA

2009

FAFA SUPERMALL
GUANGZHOU, CHINA

CENTRE DEUX
ST. ETIENNE, FRANCE

DAMING PALACE NATIONAL HERITAGE PARK DEVELOPMENT
XI'AN, CHINA

METALLIST CITY CENTRE
KHARKIV, UKRAINE

2010

NANJING TAIWAN TRADE MART
NANJING, CHINA

MARINA CITY
QINGDAO, CHINA

WALSIN D
NANJING, CHINA

HERCULES DOWNTOWN URBAN FRAMEWORK
HERCULES, CALIFORNIA

IN CONSTRUCTION

NIEUW HOOG CATHARIJNE
UTRECHT, THE NETHERLANDS

MOSKVA COLLECTION
MOSCOW, RUSSIA

GALLERIA STONECZNA
RADOM, POLAND

TORONTO UNION STATION
TORONTO, CANADA

WALSIN CENTRO AB
NANJING, CHINA

WALSIN VILLAGE C1/C2
NANJING, CHINA

WUHAN SHIMAO CARNIVAL
WUHAN, CHINA

HAPPY VALLEY
GUANGZHOU, CHINA

WORLD TRADE CENTER
WENZHOU, CHINA

FAR EASTERN
TAICHUNG, TAIWAN

IN DESIGN / CONCEPT

LUNG CHEUNG
HONG KONG

KAI TIN
HONG KONG

VICTORIA CITY
BUCHAREST, ROMANIA

MIXED-USE PROJECT
AMSTERDAM, THE NETHERLANDS

MIXED-USE PROJECT
ROTTERDAM, THE NETHERLANDS

DALIAN VIVO CENTER
DALIAN, CHINA

WALSIN MIXED-USE COMPLEX
JINAN, CHINA

ZHENGZHOU
ZHENGZHOU, CHINA

TIANJIN MIXED-USE
TIANJIN, CHINA

SHENYANG MIXED-USE
SHENYANG, CHINA

KUNMING MIXED-USE
KUNMING, CHINA

FUZHOU MIXED-USE
FUZHOU, CHINA

CHANGSHA MIXED-USE
CHANGSHA, CHINA

HU TAI LU MIXED-USE
SHANGHAI, CHINA

PROJECT INDEX

Hollywood & Highland, Los Angeles, California **60**
Client: TrizecHahn Development Corporation, San Diego
Transit Authority: Los Angeles County Metropolitan Transportation
Authority (Metro)
Executive Architect: Altoon + Porter Architects LLP
Retail Architect: Ehrenkranz, Eckstut & Kuhn Architects
Theatre Interior Design Architect: Rockwell Group
Hotel Architect: Wimberly Allison Tong & Goo (WATG)
Landscape Architect: Rios Associates
Project Completion: 2001
Size: 1,200,000 SF GLA (111,483 SM GLA), 2-Level Open-Air
Shopping Center
Cost: $430 m

Toronto Union Station, Toronto, Ontario, Canada **64**
Client: Redcliff Realty Management, Inc. and City of Toronto
Transit Authority: Toronto Transit Commission
Prime Design Architect & Engineers: NORR Limited
Retail Consultant: Altoon + Porter Architects LLP
Heritage Architect: Fournier Gersovitz Moss & Associés
Project Completion: Currently in construction

Centrum Chodov, Prague, Czech Republic **68**
Client: Rodamco Ceska Republika Multi Development Corporation,
Gouda, The Netherlands
Transit Authority: Prague Metro, Prague Public Transit Company
Client In-House Concept: T+T
Architect of Record: A-2000
Design Completion: Fall 2003
Size: 678,126 SF (63,000 SM) shopping center over 4-levels

Metallist City Centre, Kharkiv, Ukraine **72**
Client: CP Capital Partners, Toronto; DCDH, Kiev, Ukraine
Transit Authority: Moskovsky Metropoliten
Size: 807,293 SF (75,000 SM) on four levels

Moskva Collection, Moscow, Russia **76**
Client: OJSC "DecMos", Moscow
Transit Authority: Moscow Metro
Design Completion: 2006
Size: 1,076,391 SF (100,000 SM) on 3-levels plus cinema

Victoria City, Bucharest, Romania **80**
Client: Victoria City Entertainment and Shopping Center SRL with
CD Capital Partners, Toronto
Transit Authority: Bucharest Metro
Local Architect: B23T Architecture Studio
Project/Design Completion: 2011
Size: 936,460 SF (87,000 SM) GBA on 3-levels

Mucha Centre, Prague, Czech Republic **84**
Client: European Property Development (EPD)
Transit Authority: Prague Public Transit Company
Design Competition Completion: 1999
Size: 1,400,000 SF (130,064 SM)

Gresham Station, Gresham, Oregon **88**
Client: Winmar/Safeco, Seattle
Transit Authority: TriMet MAX Light Rail and TriMet Bus
Design Completion: Winter 1989
Size: 850,000 SF (78,967SM) GLA

Walsin Mixed-use Complex, Jinan, China **94**
Client: Walsin
Transit Authority: Jinan Metro
Associate Architect Consultant: Archasia Design Group
Concept Designer: Altoon + Porter Architects LLP
Design Completion: 2011
Size: 15,695,406 SF GBA (1,458,141 SM GBA), which
includes 1,815,494 SF (168,665 SM) commercial GLA and
1,241,423 SF (115,332 SM) residential

TRANSIT ADJACENT DEVELOPMENT

CentralWorld, Bangkok, Thailand **100**
Client: Central Pattana (CPN), Bangkok
Transit Authority: Bangkok Mass Transit System Public Company Limited
Local Architect of Record: A49
Local Landscape Architect: L49
Local Interior Architect: IA49
Project Completion: 2007
Size: 2,000,495 SF (185,852 SM)
Awards: 2009 ICSC Asia Design & Development Award and 2010 ICSC
Global VIVA! Best-of-the-Best Award

PROJECT INDEX

Nieuw Hoog Catharijne, Utrecht, The Netherlands **108**
Client: Corio Nederland Retail BV, Utrecht (overall development) and ING
Real Estate Development (residential)
Transit Authority: Nederlandse Spoorwegen (NS) Rail
Architect of Record: Van Den Oever Zaaijer & Partners
Project Completion: Currently in Construction
Size: 3,767,368 SF (350,000 SM)

The Shops at Tanforan, San Bruno, California **114**
Client: Wattson Breevast , Irvine, CA/Amsterdam, The Netherlands
Transit Authority: Bay Area Rapid Transit (BART)
Project Completion: October 2005
Size: 1,041,000 SF (96,712 SM) GLA

The Atrium at Kursky Station, Moscow, Russia **118**
Client: Engeocom, Moscow
Transit Authority: Moscow Metro
Project Completion: Summer 2002
Size: 280,000 SF (26,012 SM) urban infill, featuring fashion retail,
entertainment, and education facilities

Yasenevo, Moscow, Russia **122**
Client: Simon-Ivanhoe, Paris and OST Group, Moscow
Transit Authority: Moscow Metro
Associate Architect: MosProject - 2
Design Completion: 2005
Size: 1,636,114 SF (152,000 SM) over two levels of retail, entertainment
and recreation and four to six levels of office over retail

Wuhan Shimao Carnival, Wuhan, China **126**
Client: Shimao Group, Shanghai
Transit Authority: Wuhan Metro
Associate Architect Consultant: Archasia Design Group
Architect of Record: LDI
Project/Design Completion: 2011
Size: 5,381,955 SF (500,000 SM) entertainment/retail center designed
around a 65,000 SM amusement park, a man-made lagoon, with
2 waterfront service apartments and a five-star hotel

Buchanan Galleries, Glasgow, Scotland **130**
Client: Buchanan Partnership, Slough Estates
Transit Authority: Glasgow Subway, Strathclyde Partnership for Transport
Design Completion: 2004
Size: 400,100 SF (37,170 SM) GLA

TRANSIT ENVIRONMENT DEVELOPMENT

Brno Campus Square, Brno, Czech Republic **136**
Client: AIG Lincoln, Czech Republic
Transit Authority: Brno Municipal Public Transport (DPMB a.s.)
Architect of Record: A-Plus
Project Completion: 2008
Size: 269,097 SF (25,000 SM) GLA

Mozaika (Third Ring), Moscow, Russia **140**
Clients: Simon Ivanhoe, Paris and OST Group, Moscow
Transit Authority: Moscow Metro
Associate Architects: MosProject 2 and Spectrum
Design Completion: 2008
Size: 1,442,364 SF (134,000 SM) on 3-levels

Monash Village Caulfield Campus, Melbourne, Australia **144**
Client: Equiset—Grollo Group
Transit Authority: Metlink
Architect of Record: NH Architecture
Heritage Architect: Bryce Raworth
Design Completion: 2004
Size: 41,979 SF (3,900 SM) supermarket; 37,673 SF (3,500 SM) specialty
retail; 436 student apartments; 118,403 SF (11,000 SM) office space;
45,208 SF (4,200 SM) education space
Project Value: $300 m

The LOOP, Ghent, Belgium **148**
Client: NV Grondbank The Loop
Transit Authority: De Lijn
Design Completion: 2007
Size: 5,947,060 SF (552,500 SM) office, retail, leisure, residential and expo extension

Daming Palace National Heritage Park Development, Xi'an, China **152**
Client: Xi'an Qujiang Daming Palace Investment Group, LTD
Transit Authority: Xi'an Metro/Xi'an Municipal People's Government
Design Completion: 2009
Size: 1,076,391 SF (100,000 SM) Retail, Food & Beverage Gallery, Museum and Cultural Facilities

TRANSIT INDUCING DEVELOPMENT

Charleroi Station Hub Master Plan, Brussels, Belgium **158**
Client: Equilis, Brussels and PP&A
Transit Authority: Charleroi Pre-metro, TEC (Transport En Commun)
Associate Architect: Paul Petit & Associés
Design Completion: 2008

Fashion Valley Center, San Diego, California **162**
Client: Lend Lease Real Estate Investments, Inc. (Formerly ERE, Yarmouth Inc.)
Transit Authority: San Diego Metropolitan Transit System
Project/Design Completion: Fall 1997
Size: 1,691,887 SF (157,181 SM) GLA
Awards: 1999 ICSC International Design & Development Award

DEVELOPMENT INDUCING TRANSIT

Marina City, Qingdao, China **168**
Client: Qingdao Tai Shan Real Estate Co., LTD, Qingdao
Transit Authority: Qingdao Metro
Associate Architect: Archasia Design Group
Project Completion: Spring 2010
Size: 1,076,391 SF (100,000 SM) waterfront marketplace on 3-Levels above grade, 1 level retail below

Redmond Town Center, Redmond, Washington **174**
Client: Winmar/Safeco, Seattle
Transit Authority: King County Metro Transit
Design Completion: 1986
Size: 1,400,000 SF (130,064 SM) on 120 acres
Cost: $70 m (estimated)

PHOTOGRAPHY/RENDERING CREDITS

Albert Lim KS: Sengkang MRT Station, Buangkok MRT Station

Ales Lezatka: Brno Campus Square

Carlos Diniz Associates: Redmond Town Center (Architectural Illustrations)

Compas Atelier: Victoria City (Renderings)

Da-Code Design: Monash Village Caulfield Campus (Renderings)

David Hewitt/Ann Garrison – David Hewitt/Ann Garrison Architectural Photography: Fashion Valley Center

DP Studio Co., LTD: Mozaika (Third Ring) (Renderings)

DPI Animation House: New Hoog Catharijne (Renderings)

Erhard Pfeiffer – Erhard Pfeiffer Photography: Fashion Valley Center

Grant Sheehan Photography: Botany Town Centre

Greg Keating, AIA: Hollywood & Highland, The Shops at Tanforan, Fashion Valley Center, Moskva Collection

Hockenberger and Associates: Gresham Station (Architectural Illustrations)

Ian Espinoza Associates: The Atrium at Kursky Station (Architectural Illustration)

Marc Gerritsen Photography: Nanjing Taiwan Trade Mart, Marina City

NORR Limited: Toronto Union Station (Architectural Watercolor Illustrations)

QingYuan Computer Graphics Co., LTD: Walsin Centro AB (Renderings), Walsin Village C1/C2 (Renderings), Nanjing Taiwan Trade Mart (Rendering), Wuhan Shimao Carnival (Renderings), Yasenevo (Renderings), Walsin Mixed-use Complex (Renderings)

QuickiT: Charleroi Station Hub Master Plan

Radka Ciglerová: Centrum Chodov

Scott Lockard: Kowloon Station (Architectural Illustrations)

Shadow Map Digital Graphics Co., LTD: Daming Palace National Heritage Park Development (Renderings), Marina City (Rendering)

Transparent House: Metallist City Centre (Renderings)

Ukit Hanamonset: Central World

Wayne Thom: The Shops at Tanforan